OUR WORLD
ECONOMIC AND POLITICAL PROJECTIONS
PART 1

RAMESH RAIZADA

CREATE SPACE
An Amazon Company

Acknowledgements
I want to express my gratitude to my wife Rekha, my daughter Nishi and my son Avinash for their love and understanding.
We all know that writing any book requires dedication and enthusiasm; for that there is no better place than our own family and well wishers. This book is dedicated to you. I want to thank the staff of Create Space for their valuable technical help in publishing Our World; my heartfelt thanks to my friends and loyal readers.

CONTENTS

Preface

The world is changing and the speed is fast; it is so heartening to see that the change is in the right direction. It is optimistic, more stable and dynamic. There are no signs of dark clouds, hovering over our planet Earth that loomed prominently sixty years ago. It seems that gentle and soft breeze is passing through our midst, at this juncture in our lives. It is a good sign to see that not only the majority of the people but also the leadership of the world is on the same page in terms of perception and direction for the world to follow. Domination, conversion from theirs to our way has lost the credibility and acceptance. In lieu, co-existence, appreciation, and tolerance have emerged. This is a better World which is emerging fast and it is finding stronger roots among the majority of the people all over the world.

When there is peace and trust among countries, people could think of improvements, making their lives more interesting, challenging and more productive. Science and technology would force us to adopt better ways of doing things in our lives. When the focus in our lives is to build a better world for all of us rather than for few, when we see the whole planet as our own part, when the happiness and prosperity is not limited to privileged few, it is bound to spell out practical, acceptable, universal, fair and legitimate, way of doing things. Business would thrive; there would be more connectivity between the people, there would be more social, cultural and intellectual sharing of ideas. That is good.

Given those above mentioned conditions, we shall put our thoughts and analytical research to see how our world would look like in the near future say five years from now. We are talking in terms of upcoming trends in economic conditions, our eating habits housing preferences, fashion in clothing, dresses, transportation modes, social activities, working opportunities, travelling choices, inter connectivity, religious tolerances and all gamut that form our modern day living.

We shall begin with Economic and Political Analysis of different countries, regions along with global trends starting from Asia. We shall touch basis first with the most prominent countries and then move on to other countries of the region. We have selected twenty countries from Asia, Europe and America in our present study, Part 1; the other countries will be included in Part 2.

Our world is getting smaller; more connected than ever before. Vibrant changes are taking place in all realms of our lives everyday. Dramatic make over in politics, economic environments and cultural activities have taken the central stage of our world. We are witnessing a mammoth collusion of fast moving elements of kinetic energy in all directions. The new beginning of the twenty first century is going to be a harbinger of great technological advances and fast changes in all communities of our society. We are moving on in the right direction.

We have undertaken this important task, in our study to explore, examine and analyze the political, economic and cultural aspects connected with our lives, as they exist, at this time, in different countries of the world. As mentioned above, we have selected twenty countries of Europe, Asia and America in Part 1 of our study. We consider these countries very important and potential trend setters. These countries are: China, Japan, India, South Korea, Indonesia, Thailand, Malaysia, Philippines, Pakistan,

Australia, Germany, France, United Kingdom, Italy, Russia, Turkey, United States, Canada, Mexico and Brazil.

When we look at a country from political point of view, we have to see different entities of political structure; starting from the type of the government- is it a full fledged democratic country or is it run by a ruthless dictator? Furthermore, there could be some countries which may be lying in between these two systems. We have to demarcate between ideologies, too. Is it a Communist country or there is, some thriving Capitalism? We have to look at stability of the government and peaceful environment in the country. It is of paramount importance. Companies do not put their money for investment unless they feel that the money is safe. Social and political unrest in a country would discourage internal as well as foreign investor. After 9/11 episode, we hear a lot about Al Qaeda and Taliban; Islamic militants are causing havoc in many countries like Afghanistan and Pakistan. We have to make a note of these conditions and bring out clearly the prevailing factors for each country under our study.

There are only few countries where corruption at the top political leadership is not only considered beneath dignity but is discouraged and punished severely. When a president or prime minister of a country starts taking bribery or pocket money for his own good, how could we expect that country to make progress? Many of the emerging countries of the world have fallen victim of this hidden agenda and unfortunately this horrendous problem of stealing wealth from the nation can not be ruled out completely. However, it could be said with certainty that corruption at any level of the government structure is bound to take the country down and the future would be dark. We have to collect this vital information for each country in details.

Like any business organization, countries go up or down depending upon the caliber of the national leadership. It is the catalyst for change and progress. Without Vision and dreams and clear cut plans, a country can not move exponentially. At the same token, plans written on papers if not executed with efficiency could result in chaos and waste of precious resources. It has been seen that politicians make big speeches and loud propaganda about their plans to please the public but at the end of the day they mean nothing. We have to sort out those countries where this has become a norm. The country stays put, does not move and the leaders go scot free and unharmed. Truly quoted, sizzling progress goes parallel to fired up leadership of a country.

In our changing world, alliances and fraternities between different countries carry a substantial global influence. Since World War I to the present times, many countries have shifted their positions but there are some which remained united, like a solid rock, in all the adverse situations. The best example of this relationship is that of the United States and the United Kingdom. It must be pointed out explicitly that countries change their alliances based upon the existing conditions; national interest become the number one priority criteria, in almost all the cases. The political scenario of any country is governed by changes that keep cropping in from time to time. However certain fundamentals remain in tact. Twenty years ago how many countries were affected by the presence of Al Qaeda? Now, the whole world bears its imprint.

Politics and Economics are two defining factors for any country; they are closely interconnected. It is the wealth of a country which is translated into Gross Domestic Product which in turn defines prosperity or poverty in a nation. Gross National Income is directly linked to the population of the country. When we look at any country we look at these two leading indicators. The wealth created in any country depends upon many well laid out systems and business environments. How the national government treats the foreign investor in terms of incentives, tax breaks, remittance of money and duty free environment-these are some of the leading inducements which are necessary for achieving higher national growth. Pro business policies for internal as well as for outsiders, are essential to create an atmosphere for sustained forward momentum. Transparency in governing bodies, condition of infrastructure, a pool of educated and technically trained workforce, fair labor laws, reliable judicial system and fast moving bureaucratic organizations, are pre requisites for a well laid out economic structure. Banking and Credit policies carry a heavy weight to increase the production of goods and services.

In 2008, United States economy almost collapsed; recession hit 1930 scenario. Many leading banks failed which sent jitters to the whole world. Wars in Afghanistan and Iraq guzzled up American wealth. Other leading countries like England, France, Germany and Japan were facing the same kind of economic turmoil and the picture looked bleak. High unemployment, deep national deficits and negative growth had put countries in deep trouble. It took few years when the picture started to look better. Billions of dollars were spent by various government agencies to prop up the economy. Gradually the global economy turned the corner and things are looking better, now. During this recession time, the Chinese economy remained steady and in fact gave a big support to turn the corner around. Credit must be given to the Chinese leadership to reestablish a healthy global economy. This serious economic disaster reminds us once again that our world is very much interconnected and it is a very important responsibility of all the leading nations to work together and take necessary actions so that we do not face such a catastrophic situation again.

When we scan the economies of different countries, certain characteristics of political leadership, business sharpness of few individuals or organizations, availability of capital and trained workforce stand as the most powerful motivating factors to move a country on a sustained high level trajectory. The common man, a person on the bottom of the pyramid does not drive the economic cycle of a nation; it is the top leadership that takes the control. A fired up, dedicated, intelligent and visionary person of high caliber at the top can make it or break it. Half hearted or hesitant leadership can not steer the ship with speed and glorious results. The most outstanding recognition in this respect should go to the Chinese leadership model. For a communist country to do such an outstanding job is worth noting down. It also shows the powerful force of capitalism when it is followed with vigor and uncanny diligence. India and other developing nations would highly benefit from the show case examples of the bold Chinese plans.

When we have a person like Steve Jobs at the top, a company has nowhere to go except to the highest perfection; it holds so good in case of any country likewise. The economic condition of any country depends upon the caliber of the governing elite, their determination, their sharp economic and financial understanding and dedication to make things happen. Government policies regarding taxation, public expenditure, job creation, growth plans and rooting out corruption and waste have to be given the highest priorities. A developing country is different from a developed nation; hence the tools to change have to be different. So are the goals and objectives as well as the pace.

Energizing the economy by pumping billions of dollars as stimulant funds, letting the national debt go little bit higher and borrowing from International institutions would not doom the prospects of higher national growth provided every thing is executed with splendid precision and full control. Top class infrastructure along with first class higher education universities propels the economic growth faster. In our study, we have looked at these existing conditions in different countries and have provided some reasonable projections. It has also been established that new blood has to be infused in a society to move it faster. The main objective of our study has been to look and analyze the existing data on economy and the political leadership presiding in the country. The selected twenty countries provide a reasonable good sample of the top to the bottom categories in terms of sizzling growth and visionary movement to a sagging economy and deplorable leadership. Our efforts had been to be fair and accurate in making judgment when it came to draw future projections. In all these kinds of studies, some discretionary opinions and views do creep into; however the major thrust is not dented.

After World War II, the most important event that took place was the end of the cold war that was raging between Russia and the western world for few decades. The disintegration of the United Soviet Socialist Republic (USSR) in 1991 paved the way for peaceful relations between the United States and Russia. In 1949, China entered the global scene and now is the leading contender to become a Super Power. In not too distant future, it will start calling shots which could not be ignored.

Population plays a dominant role in making a country prosperous or mired in poverty. Most of the Scandinavian countries have a low population of five to ten million people but at the same token they are educated and technically well trained. These are two pluses in their favor. Most of the Asian countries, on the other hand are densely populated and the education and technical competency parts are missing. It will take a long time before this situation would change in Asia and Africa.

Entrepreneurship is a leading factor for taking a country forward; the United States of America has shown the world what it could achieve with this dominant asset. Every body knows about Silicon Valley Effect. Micro financing, especially in Asian countries, has assumed a prominent role in sprouting budding new entrepreneurs. The caliber of political leadership in any country dictates the economic climate for that nation. This fundamental rule is very important to establish a thriving democratic set up and transparency in governing institutions. We have followed these basic cardinal principles in our analysis.

INTRODUCTION
SELECTED TWENTY COUNTRIES
China

The second largest economy of the world with a Gross Domestic Product over eight trillion dollars, is moving fast in all areas of human activities. Chinas population is 1.3 Billions (2013), the largest populated country in the world. It has the largest numbers of multi-millionaires and billionaires in Asia. However, the Gross National Income is very low compared to highly developed countries of Europe because of huge population; two to three hundred million people are below the poverty level-making less than a dollar a day in wages. There is a tremendous gap between the rich and the poor.

The above data shows that the elite group of the country can easily afford to buy the most expensive items-luxury homes, sports cars, designer's dresses and costly dinners and lunches. The rural family however, is still struggling with poverty and deprivation. The Chinese government is taking steps to decrease this imbalance between the rich and the poor but it will take sometime before that happens. The way the Chinese economy is moving, it will be correct to assume that millions will be lifted out of poverty level within five years or so. It is a great credit to the Chinese government and lessons should be learnt by other developing countries of Asia, South America and Africa.

Mega cities like Beijing, Shanghai and Hong Kong would be taking the places of Paris and London with all glories of latest fashion and exclusiveness. The growth in China would bring out more of modern, Euro-Asian culture, inter mingling with the best of the both world in terms of economic emancipation and general standard of living. The common man and woman of China would be better off economically in the coming five years .All the trends

11

are showing upward movement towards greater prosperity. It seems like that China would keep up the movement for growth till it hits the slowing syndrome because of internal exhaustion. China might be fashioning itself on the Japanese model in the long run. The Economic Projections for China are solidly positive.

Japan: The third largest economy of the world is Japan. The Gross Domestic Product is over five trillions. The population of Japan is over one hundred millions and it is in the decline mode. Japan is a developed country; its Gross National Income is comparable to the countries of Western Europe-around 38K. Highly industrialized with a firm footing in latest technology, Japan is the only Asian country which has developed into a first class economic Super power. The land of the rising sun, Nippon or Japan has gone into a deep recession, lately and many economists have projected some dismal pictures for the country. The foreign exchange reserves are second to China; however, a combination of internal inertia and some external economic factors have forced the Japanese economy to a stand still position. Some analysts have named the present economy as a lost decade for the country.

The present Prime-Minister of Japan Mr.Abe is telling the world that he is going to reverse this trend by pumping billions of dollars in Stimulus packing for accelerating personal spending as well as making improvements in infrastructure. It is important to note that the Japanese economy is important for the overall well being of the global prosperity .The coming two years in Japanese industry would give us good indications whether the country will be coming out of deflation and recession or would be stuck in deeper troubles. Will it bring further contraction in Japanese business world wide or expand to greater height, it is difficult to predict. It would affect many countries of East Asia notably China, South Korea, Indonesia and Australia. Japanese economic trends, most probably would move up. Stimulus program looks encouraging.

India: The third largest economy of Asia is India. Like China, India has a very large population-1.2 Billions. The Gross Domestic Product is around 1.8 trillions. The Gross National Income is very low because of the huge population; more than four hundred million people are below poverty line. At the same time, India does have a hefty slice of three hundred million people who could be classified as middle class. In the past few years, the country was moving with a spectacular growth of eight percent per year. However, the growth has slowed down to five percent in 2014. Serious recession in the United States and Europe has changed this picture. The Economic Projections for India is positively upward; the growth may be slow, around 5% of GDP.

South Korea: The fourth largest economy of Asia is South Korea. It has a population of fifty million people and the Gross National Income is around $28K per capita. South Korea can boast of some of the most successful companies of the world like Samsung, Hyundai, LG, Kia and others. South Korean economy has really turned out to be very dynamic like the old Japanese model. Presently however, like other economies of Asia, South Korea is experiencing a little bit of slow movement in its economy- down to 2.3%. But there are no signs of recession. Japan, China, United States, Australia and other countries would assure South Korean business to keep moving up. With more disposable income available to a large group of people, South Korean economic picture looks good in the next five years.

Indonesia: It is the largest Muslim country of the world with a population around 250 million people. During the regime of Military dictator Suharto, Indonesia made good progress in terms of economic growth and industrialization. The Gross National Income per capita is roughly four thousand dollars per year. The present President of the country General Yudhoyono is the first democratically elected President of Indonesia. The country is moving forward economically but not with a fast pace. Too much corruption and other important factors are holding the country to a slower pace of forward movement in terms of overall standard of living for the average Indonesian. A slow progression is predicted.

Thailand: It is the only country of Asia which was never dominated by any European power. It is a Buddhist country; population of seventy million people. The Gross National Income is five thousand dollars per capita per year. Monarchy, Military establishment and Buddhism govern the daily life of a Thailand citizen. Thailand is a very popular destination of tourists from all over the world. Some of the most beautiful temples of the world adorn the capital city of Bangkok. The present Prime-Minister of Thailand is Yingluck Shinawatra, the younger sister of former Prime-Minister. She is very popular with the rural working class and women in particular. There is a big question mark about her competency in leading the country to higher growth and sustained prosperity. There is plenty of room for Thailand to grow in all areas of business activities.

Malaysia: It is a country of thirty million people; sixty percent are Muslims. The Gross National Income is twelve thousand dollars per capita per year. The twenty five percent Chinese population of the country is the most affluent group of the society. Most of the business community comprises of Chinese people. However, the country is being run by the native Malaysian citizens; so tension exists between different cross sections of the society. Malaysia is rich in oil and it has good potentials to grow, economically. Right now the extreme militant group of Muslims does not have big appeal among the masses. Economy will move up marginally but no spectacular growth is foreseen in the near future.

Philippines: The country has good potentials to provide a better standard of living for its citizens. Unfortunately, it has not been realized for some reasons. The main causes are high level of corruption, non competency to govern the country and lack of motivation to move forward. There is a huge outflow of educated and talented people to other countries because there are very few opportunities of gainful employment locally. The economic conditions of the country would improve only if there is a dynamic leadership in the country. The present President of Philippines is the son of former President Cory Aquino; he has promised to end the corruption cycle in the government but no big changes have been sighted. If the top leadership is committed to change and takes strong actions, there is no reason for Philippines not to move towards strong economic plateau; the world is moving fast towards greater progress and prosperity and Philippines can achieve it.

Pakistan: Islamic Republic of Pakistan is a sad story of government failure. The country has become a hotbed of every day bomb explosions, innocent killing, extremism, terrorism, lack of tolerance for other religions and home of Taliban and Al Qaeda However, it should be pointed out that Pakistan is a Nuclear Power and consequently it carries a powerful voice. The economic conditions, in the mean time, have gone worse from bad. New elections are supposed to take place in May 2013 and that might change the situation of Pakistan .Note: New elections have taken place and it is hoped that the new government would change the economic conditions for the country and its citizens.

Australia: One of the most prosperous and advanced countries of the world, Australia has a population of twenty three million people. The Gross National Income per capita is $56K per year. Ninety percent of the population is Caucasian; the majority is from England and Ireland. The queen of England is also the head of the Australian government. The major trading partners are China, Japan, United States and England; the country is rich in Uranium, Iron and liquid petroleum gas. Australian Universities have become a good resource for earning foreign currencies. Sydney and Melbourne have attracted sizeable number of Chinese and Indian students. The country has a bright future ahead; the economic growth is around 2-3% per annum. Australian economy is not fully dependent on European and U. S economy; Chinese, Indian, Korean and Japanese business carries more weight .There are no visible sighs of any recession at this moment; we can project a robust growth for Australian economy.

We shall now consider some of the major countries of Europe; how these countries are doing now and how they are going to move in the next five years in terms of economic progression. The economic prosperity of Europe is dictated by countries like Germany, France, England and Italy. Portugal, Spain, Ireland and Greece are facing tough times.

Germany: The largest economy of Europe is Germany. It has the population of 82 million people. The Gross National Income is 44K per capita per year. It is the second largest exporting country in the world; well known for quality products. It is the country of famous musicians, political philosophers (Karl Marx: Das Capita propounded theory of Communism) and world class Scientists and Scholars. With three trillion dollars, Gross Domestic Product, Germany is the fourth largest economy of the world. Recession in European countries especially in Greece, Spain and Portugal has forced International Monetary Fund and Germany to bail out these countries from financial disaster. German Chancellor Angela Merkel is a strong supporter of financial stability within Eurozone; it is causing some resentful reactions from the German voters. Technically smart and hard working Germans have transformed their country from the ruins of World War II.

France: This is the country famous for its wine and cheese, not to underscore the fashion industry. A country of 63 million people, its economy is the second largest in Europe with 2.6 trillion dollars Gross Domestic Product. The Gross National Income is 43K per capita per year. The land of Liberty, Equality and Justice is a thriving democracy. France and Germany are strong supporters of European Community and are helping out financially strapped economies of Europe like Greece, Spain and others. France has a big military force; a nuclear power. The overall economic growth is not spectacular but not stagnant; range is 1.5-2.5% per annum. The recently elected Socialist President Mr.Hollande is going to promote socialistic programs which might benefit the common man and woman of France.

United Kingdom: Queen Elizabeth is the head of State not only of England but, that of Australia, Canada and fourteen other sovereign countries too. She is very popular and one of the richest women of the world. The present population of the United Kingdom is 63 millions strong. It has a Gross National Product of 2.4 trillions and the National Income per capita is 38K per year. At one point in time, England virtually ruled all over the world. Things have changed now; very recently Brazil has taken over the United Kingdom's place as the sixth largest economy of the world. At the end of World War II, United States became the most powerful country in the world, economically and militarily. It took over the place of England and other European countries. During the last two to four years (2008-2012), the economy of England has been moving erratically, mostly downwards. The effect of worldwide recession is being felt by the government and the common man on the street. The present Prime Minister of England, David Cameron, a Conservative, has slashed government spending and reduced or eliminated many social programs to balance the budget deficits. The economy is chugging along.

Italy: When we talk about Italy, we are talking about Rome, Venice and Florence; gorgeous beautiful cities. We are also mentioning the names of Michelangelo and Leonardo da Vinci, the world renowned artists. Italy is also famous for its wine and Pasta. The present conditions in the country are not rosy; it is facing severe Public debt crisis. Corruption and Mafia influence has sapped the country's growth. Italy has a population of 60 million people and it is the third largest economy of Eurozone with a Gross Domestic Product over two trillion dollars. The National Income is

35K per capita per year. The country is well known for beautifully designed products -sports cars, dresses and other consumer products. The richest citizen of the country is Silvio Berlusconi; the two time Prime-Minister who happened to be involved in sex scandal and other corruption charges.

Russia: Once a Super power, Russia is facing an uphill battle to become an economic power house. From the point of view of Military strength, Space and Nuclear Technology, Russia is still a leading force. It is the largest country of the world in terms of area; it has a population of 142 million strong. It has a low life expectancy of 65 years for male and 73 years for female. Russia is rich in Oil and Gas but it has not been able to build strong business structure. The Gross National Income is 11k per capita which is very much less compared to other west European countries. The country has not been able to set up a thriving business environment and there is inertia, corruption and incompetency in running the government. A member of BRICS (Brazil, Russia, India, China and South Africa) it has a Gross Domestic Product of 1.5 Trillion dollars. Russia is one of the largest military equipment exporting countries; China and India are the major buyers of Russian military hardware. Russian economy depends upon the Global Gas and Oil prices. Unlike China, Russia is not a driving economic force. It does no command any big political influence in the world anymore. A slow growth is projected for Russia.

Turkey: This is the country among all Muslim countries of the world which may be called highly westernized and not influenced by Islamic militants. It has a population of 74 million people and the Gross National Income is $11K per capita. It has the second largest military force in NATO (North Atlantic Treaty Organization). It has good relations with the United States and other European Nations. Turkey is a good role model for other Muslim countries. The military is no more a dictating force but still a very powerful unit in running the government machinery.

We shall now look at some of the most important countries of North and South America. These countries are the leaders in setting the economic trends in the world. United States of America, Canada, Brazil, Mexico and Argentina would play important roles in changing the world economy.

United States: The only Super Power of the world boasts an economy of about 16 Trillion dollars; it has a population of 320 million people. The Gross Domestic Income is$50K per capita per year. It is the greatest military power; the defense budget of the United States is equal to the combined total military budgets of all the countries of the world. One fourth of total economic production of the world takes place in the United States. With these astounding statistics, no wonder United States can dictate its terms and conditions to the rest of the world. A country where individualism and entrepreneurship is at the top of the list of human endeavor, it seems that no other country would come close to its achievements until the conditions change dramatically. It has been said that China might overtake United States in two to three decades from now-around 2050 or so. It seems to us that China like Japan might run into difficulties of one kind or the other and the Chinese dream might never be achieved. It would be interesting though to watch, how things move along. It is the United States economy that propels the economies of the world, period. United States is the leading charger of consumerism. It is very much true that the world gets stalled when the United States stops to move. It is therefore very much important to see the American economy move forward. The recent recession (2008-2012) has jolted and shook the rosy picture of United States. Wars in Iraq and Afghanistan, waged by the United States, were very big blunders. Thousands of innocent lives were lost for ever and billions of dollars got wasted on engaging in these fruitless wars. It will take courageous and bold steps to bring the economy to its lost glory. President Obama seems to be moving in the right direction but lot of work has to done to bring the economy to its past glorious stature which was witnessed during President Clinton's presidency. If the Republican Party keeps putting up road blocks for President Obama, it will be difficult to achieve tangible results. The world is watching; Republicans have lost the touch.

Canada: Canada is the second largest country of the world; the population is only 34 million people. It is a rich country with Gross National Income of 45K per capita. United States and Canada are the largest trading partners. Both countries are partners of North America Free Trading Agreement (NAFTA). The Gross Domestic Product is 1.8 Trillion dollars. Canada recognizes Queen Elizabeth as Head of the State. Quebec is now given a special status as autonomous nation within Canada. French and English are the official languages of Canada. It is rich in oil and Gas. Unlike United States which went through Bank failures in the recent recession (2008-2012), Canadian banks did a pretty good job. Canada has a great potential of taking higher position in global politics if it increase its population and build a large military base. The present Prime-Minister of Canada, Steven Harper is trying to enlarge the trading partnership with China and India. The economic outlook for Canada is very positive.

Mexico: It is a country of the rich as well as poor; the richest man of the world comes from Mexico. It has a population of 116 million people. The Gross National Income is $10K per capita. Mexico is rich in Oil and Gas; Mayan civilization flourished before the Spanish conquered the land. It is a member of NAFTA. Unfortunately, drug lords rule over the country and the safety of life is not guaranteed. Because of much better economic conditions in the United States, millions of illegal Mexican citizens take the risk and cross the border line to come to United States. A permanent wall has been built along the border line to stop the migration but it is not effective. Mexican economy depends quite a bit on money transfer from the Mexican immigrants living in the

United States. If the country has to make good economic progress, it has to get rid of the drug trafficking and corruption in the government. The United States government has been helping the Mexican government to eliminate the drug cartels who have established themselves in a very strong position. Looking from these existing scenarios, the outlook for Mexican economy to grow on a strong footing does not look bright. There is lot of poverty in the country and political leadership is not competent to transform the basic structure of the government. That is the problem.

Brazil: A country of almost two hundred million people with a Gross National Income exceeding $10K per capita is going to host the Summer Olympic Games in 1916. This is the first time in Olympic history that a South American country is hosting the games. Brazil is endowed with plenty of iron ore deposits, grows tons of Sugar, Coffee and Oranges. Very recently, it has discovered a huge off shore oil deposits which should keep the economy growing and bring prosperity to the country. Its Gross Domestic Product has exceeded two trillion dollars which means that it is the sixth or seventh largest economy of the world.

The present president of the country is Ms Dilma Rousseff; she was the chief Assistant of President Lula de Silva. She is facing number of problems that include corruption, big divide between the rich and the poor, lack of experienced business managers, shortage of good educational institutions, large number of shanty dwelling houses called Falevas, poor infrastructure and absence of good governing structure. On a positive note, the country is not infested with drug lords; democracy is thriving and the military junta is out. Brazil is a member of emerging countries group called BRICS-Brazil, Russia, India, China and South Africa. It has the largest military force in South America; aerospace industry is strong but it is not a nuclear power. Brazil has bright future.

Analysis: Economic and Social Changes

The American Scene

United States: We shall start with the United States because it is here, that changes in all daily activities of our lives, would dictate the trends in the rest of the world. There are two distinct areas of origination of changes that take place; number one point of influx is dominated and controlled by the government and the second one resides with the general public. The leadership of the central government could, in some cases and circumstances, influence the direction and trends of the changes in the society. The changes in the behavior of the general masses would keep the momentum of changes irrespective of the government interference provided the government keeps itself away from deeper involvement. Whether it is Republican or Democratic, party, in control, in Washington D.C, fast moving changes would keep up flowing among the general masses provided the leadership in D.C does not interfere with its flow. It is very true that political leadership in the federal government could sway the general attitude of the public.

The next five years in the American history, looking from broad trends prevailing at this time, point towards liberalism and closer global interactions especially with the Asian countries. A better understanding of religious diversity and appreciation of rich Asian cultural traditions is becoming a part of American way of thinking. The younger generation of American society is getting more receptive and supportive of Asian community. This is a very positive indication of greater integration between white community and Asians. The next five years will move in this direction.

It should be noted that economic growth and full employment basket are the keys for the positive movement towards receptiveness, liberalism, openness and appreciation of other countries, communities and societies. Recession, high unemployment, unilateralism and lack of trust would have an opposite affect on global and regional cohesiveness, understanding for others and achieving common goals for the good of all. The United States of America has been a forerunner in creating millions of new jobs and advancing to greater heights of economic growth; subsequently, it could be predicted that as long as this trends last for the next five years or so, the life style of the average American would be colored and influenced by openness and receptiveness for other cultures, religious beliefs, accommodation and sharing of different views and faith in cementing new bonds with others. It would affect eating habits, craze for healthy foods, living trends, cozy but not showy homes, public versus private transportation, working places, work from home rather from established offices, dress clothes, color and style, social activities, more freedom to mix with other communities and many other features that form different rainbows of our lives.

Since more Asians especially Indians and Chinese are settling down in the United States and further more they are creating jobs in the country, local Americans are getting more open and receptive towards them. It is not true in case of Mexican migrants; they are not welcome mainly because they are not highly skilled and lack integration skills with the local communities. After 9/11 the members of the Muslim community are facing some hard times and are not trusted. Anti-American activities perpetrated by Muslim militants would radically change the Tolerance Index of the Americans. These facts are not going to change in the near future. Looking from the same perspective, Afro-Americans would continue to move up the ladder but do not expect radical changes in the society, overall. The relations with the European countries are not at the top of the American mainstream thinking; it is the global community that is taking the centerpiece. Americans and Canadians would continue to be close knitted family. The country will not move towards Conservatism; Americans would be more Liberal and open than at any other time and Asians will continue to play larger role in all areas of national growth and advancement.

The next five years will bring about many major changes in the Spanish speaking community of the country because the present leadership especially the members of the Republican party have realized the importance of reforming the immigration laws for the Mexicans. Millions of illegal immigrants would become legal citizens and that would be good for the country.

To sum up the trends of the next five years of American society, it would not be wrong to say that Americans would be moving forward towards a more open and appreciative global society.

Canadian Scenario

Canada: The second largest country of the world has a small population of only thirty four million people. It is highly industrialized and has a very high standard of living with a Gross national income approaching $45K per capita. In many ways it is a carbon copy of the United States but there are very important differences too. Canada is a distinct country of two exclusive cultures-English speaking and French. The separatist movement of French speaking population has faded off but Quebec has acquired an autonomous status within Canada.

United States of America and Canada are the largest trading partners in the global business. However, China, India and South Korea are becoming important business partners, too besides European countries. The next five years would see more interaction with Asia because Canada is a major source of oil for these countries. Not only for oil, but for various industrial products Canada could become a major trading partner of Asian countries. The present Prime-Minister of Canada Mr. Steve Harper is taking vigorous steps in that direction.

There are certain blaring differences between Canada and United States. The Banking and Financial Structure of Canada is more Conservative and nonflexible compared to the United States. During the last recession, the banking system of Canada took the heat without too much of a downturn effect on the society whereas many major banks just failed in the United States and caused lot of problems for the economy. It is a plus but it has some minus side too. During such time, it becomes very difficult to get credit from the Canadian banks and that causes problems in expansion of business transactions.

Another big difference between Canadian and United States business environment lies in the fact that Canadian Venture Capital does not take bold steps; it does not want to take un due risk in promoting business deals. The entrepreneurship in the United States is very strong and the business community backs it up without much reservation. This unique American character is missing in the Canadian business environment. It is more cautious. This may be one of the reasons that America has more multi millionaires than Canada. It is said that success comes to the bold.

Like the United States, Canada would continue to move towards Liberalism and more open society in the next five years. The Asian community would be more involved in the mainstream of Canadian landscape. For some reason or the other, the Asian community feels more at home in Canada and the United States compared to the European countries; may be because there are many common threads of culture and lesser degree of rigid norms and beliefs about Asians.

Given the size of the country and solid industrial base, Canada could scale greater heights in terms of achieving greater economical clout and global influence. It will come through liberal immigration policies that would allow more Indians, Chinese and other Asians to settle down in Canada and take the country to greater prosperity. The new highly skilled Asians are more enterprising and they create jobs. The local community is well satisfied with its prosperous environment and does not take bold steps. That means an environment of status quo-no quantum leaps-prevails. This situation can change only if there is a strong leadership vision to take the country to a global power.

Toronto and Montreal –English and French speaking cities-do provide some solid differences that exist in Canada. Though Quebec has now become an autonomous state within Canada, it seems likely that there would be more interaction between the two distinct societies; there would be more integration between the two regions. It would be good for the country as such. It seems likely that English speaking Ontario would become the heartland of Asian community. It is estimated that ten percent of Canadian population is Indians and most of them lives in Ontario and British Columbia-Toronto and Vancouver have a large community of Indians and Chinese; they have integrated very well with the local population. This trend will continue to move forward in the next five years. Surprisingly, Canada does not have a large Spanish speaking or African community. This is a very big difference between Canada and the United States.

The existing trends in social and cultural life of an average Canadian would not change drastically in the next five years. The country would become more prosperous and open to other cultures. Canada would follow its own independent foreign policy but it would synchronize with the American ground rules.

British Settings

England: The third largest economy of Europe with a Gross Domestic Product of 2.4 trillions, England has a tremendous global influence. In fashion, in music, in arts and crafts, sports and various other activities, England has played its role very well. It is the oldest democratic country and at the same time had ruled over a large section of our world. London, its capital can boast of its unique multiculturalism because people of so many countries live there. We can taste the food of Asian countries wear the Asian dresses or go to fancy European restaurant and dress up in British or European custom made clothes. Every thing is available without any hassle. We can hear the languages of the whole world in this great city of London.

The present population of England is around 62 million strong. It is not a Catholic country and the population growth is minimal but not negative. However, there is a large community of Asian and African people who have now settled down in various parts of England. The birth rate in these communities is very high and that leads to a higher population growth for the country. This trend among Asian communities will remain the same, in the next five years or so. People from all over the world want to come to England because it is still a very good place for getting a good job, health care benefits and other amenities which are not available in other parts of the world. There will be some growth in population in the local white British citizens; however, the major growth factor will come from Asians and Africans.

It is difficult to say how closely these various communities are integrated with the local population. It has been reported that in some areas there is no problem but in some places it is just the opposite. Economic conditions and education levels of the concerned community are the major factors in achieving desirable integration with the local citizens. There are people who hate or dislike Asians and Africans and there are others who are open to them and see no problem in establishing friendly relations with them. This way of thinking will persist for a long period of time; it is not going to go away soon. In this respect England is different from the United States and Canada. History, traditions, segmentation of the society into different classes and other factors such as job opportunities and Tolerance Factor come into play, here. England can not become a melting pot society; there will always be some kind of discrimination or distortion prevalent in the society especially in the lower middle class and poverty zone population. Many conservatives would not withstand the rise of non British citizens, mainly because the mentality of ruling over other people will not disappear from their way of thinking. It must be admitted however, that educated British class would mingle freely with people of other races and nationalities. That is a very big plus factor for the country to move forward.

England is very proud of maintaining its traditions; many of those traditions would remain intact but some of them would disappear too with the passing of time. Change is the only constant factor in the history of mankind; British society is not going to be different. Countries change, community change, relations change and human beings change; some do slowly and some take drastic steps. Behavior change in English society is inevitable but it would be slow and could be painful. In the next five years, we do not see any radical changes in different stratum of the British society.

The country would continue to move forward in terms of more prosperity and advancement in technology and human sciences. England may not join the European zone countries as a permanent member; it may like to take its place as a Special Member. It is true that Euro Zone is lead by Germany and France. England may not like to take a second position in this group.

Economically speaking, if England takes some clue from the American Business Model, it might replace France as the second most powerful economy of Europe. Social and Cultural changes in England would be there but will be gradual, in the next five years.

Chinese Dragon

China: The most populated country in the world with a population of 1.3 billion people has made a remarkable progress in the last thirty years. With an eight trillions Gross Domestic Product, it is now the second biggest economy of the world. The Chinese government has pulled out 300 million people from the poverty level in thirty years; it is just amazing! Communist China should be proud of its achievements. It must be noted however, that all this progress and growth has come with a price tag and that is, the freedom of the individual and enforcement of dictatorship. An agricultural country has been transformed into a global manufacturing center and it is moving forward with a tremendous force. It has been projected that within two or three decades, China would be able to compete against the United States with confidence. This projection may or may not come true; there are many important variables. Like Japan, China could encounter fatigue factors and internal economic troubles.

The recent ten years in China have seen lot of changes, economically, socially and culturally. Hundreds of millionaires have propped up but millions are still in dire poverty. There is a big divide between the urban and the rural areas. The people who have money, now travels throughout the world. It has been reported that Chinese had spent around one hundred billion dollars, last year while going on foreign vacations. They have become the largest source of giving away money to foreign countries through the net work of travel. There was a time when a similar remark was made for Japanese. But times have changed. China is flushed with abundance of money, it is acquiring more and more of Western culture; music, dresses, food and internet is dominating the Chinese culture. The life style of an urban educated executive is very much alike as that of any western country manager. Many Americans and other European citizens are now moving to China because there are more opportunities.

In terms of religious beliefs, lifestyle of every day living, eating habits and other social characteristics, an average Chinese is not moving towards a complete version of the western life. It will take a long time before a Chinese would embrace the total outfit. This could be said about other Asian countries, too. The East is east and the West is west, the twine shall meet often-that is all.

Communism does not support any religion but presently Christianity, Confucian teaching and Buddhism are flourishing in China. Strangely enough, the Chinese government is establishing many institutions which teach Confucian thoughts. Relationship between different individuals has been highlighted in his teachings; it goes back to 500 B.C; same time, when Buddha was teaching his own concepts of Nirvana. Mao was anti-religious and had nothing to do with any of these ideas. Things have changed in China, now and even Mao is no more a popular figure. Faces of new Chinese leaders have emerged in 2013. The Communist Politburo has openly declared that the number one priority for the new leaders of China would be focused on growth and military superiority. At this juncture, China lags far behind the United States and Russia in terms of military power. We do not see any open hostility between China and the U.S.A in the near future. With that understanding, we can predict that Chinese and the Americans would forge better relations, socially and culturally. More and more Chinese have started learning English language and hundreds of Chinese students enroll in the American universities, every year. There is more interaction and lesser degree of antagonism between the two nations. Chances are that this trend would continue to prevail in the near future. Two million American- Chinese who live in U.S.A, have a great influence in molding the future American Chinese relationship. It helps in cooling down the political rhetoric.

What changes we see culturally and socially in the next five years in China, are not very difficult to predict. The upper and middle class of China would embrace western way of living. The poor section of the country will gradually come out of poverty level and would continue to live Chinese way of life until it reaches the lower middle class. A foreign visitor would be able to see the old Chinese way of life as well as the modern, westernized rich upper class, existing side by side. China is trying to transform itself in a very dynamic fashion and the only thing which would stop this trend is internal fatigue factor and high level of corruption. It has been said in business circles that Chinese are very smart business operators whether they are in Thailand, Malaysia and Indonesia or in the United States.

Indian Society

India: The second most populated country in the world with a population of 1.2 billions, India may surpass China, in the near future because there is no restriction on birth control. Like China there is a wide gap between rich and the poor. There exists extreme poverty side by side with abundance of wealth. The civilizations of India and China go back to five thousand years or more. Culturally as well as socially there are many common threads between the two great countries. Economically India is far behind China with a Gross Domestic Product hovering around $1.8 trillion versus Chinese, which is $8 trillion. The chances of India catching with China are slim. Till 1962, China and India had no animosity; the relations were normal and friendly. However, after a short war in 1962, things have completely changed. There is no trust between the two countries and it might take a long time before these conditions change for the better. With out any doubt, India and China would be the leading powers in Asia.

Numerous changes have taken place in the Indian society, in recent years and they are gathering more momentum. India can boast now of a middle class of three hundred million people. Millions of people have moved out of poverty level and people in general are feeling that better times are ahead of them. Like many other Asian countries, India is a hot bed of corruption. Gone are those days when Gandhi's principles of moral endowment prevailed among the masses. The present middle class society is tuned and colored with the prevailing trends of the western culture with a tinge of Indian traditions. Indian women dresses have drastically changed and more blue jeans have taken the fashion parade. English has become more popular and American fast food chains have sprung all over the country. As the changes are seeping in the society, more heart attacks and more breast cancers are being reported in the country. It is true that most of the developing countries when they start moving up the ladder on the national scale, they acquire western way of living and abandon local traditions.

The next five years would pick up more of western style living – socially and culturally. Indian society had always been receptive to foreign ideas and ways of looking at things with different perspectives; it never had been a closed society; this will continue.

The place of a woman in the Indian society is not equal to a man; she is placed on a high pedestal but in reality she is considered a second class citizen. A man is given higher position in all aspects. Things are changing gradually-especially in urban areas but it will take a long time for the Indian woman to say that I am as good as a man. Religious taboos and traditional values are holding back Indian women; public opinion is changing but do not expect any drastic changes. An Indian woman can not put herself on the same level as an American or European woman can do. The next five years will not change this situation.

Two hundred years of British rule has already changed many facets of Indian life. After Independence, many drastic changes have taken place especially in the middle and upper stratum of Indian society. English language is getting more popular, western dresses are getting more attention and fast food is becoming the craze of the general public. Chinese food, hamburgers, fried chicken and Donuts are replacing traditional plate of Dal Roti. As in the United States, the fast food industry would thrive very well in India and this trend would continue in future.

Considering social and cultural changes in relations to other countries, the last five years show a positive trend leaning towards United States and Canada. The coming next five years or so would continue to bring about closer relations and better understanding between Indians, Americans and Canadians. The local Indians living in the States and Canada have made this change possible. They have integrated very well with the local communities and subsequently have created positive image for Indian culture. Indians are more inclined towards American and Canadian lifestyle than any other way of living. Conversely, Americans and Canadians have developed a good taste for Indian food and are interested in knowing more about Indian customs and traditions.

It is very true that this world of ours is getting flat and opening up larger vistas of different cultures and way of thinking is getting more prominent. It seems like that we are moving towards a more universal type of cultural and social world where everybody feels comfortable and consider himself/herself as a part of the whole. It is a very refreshing and enlightening experience.

Pakistan Stability

Pakistan: The country has gone through a tremendous transformation in its social and cultural life. The last ten years have changed the daily life of the ordinary citizen because the Taliban and Islamic militants have taken over the streets of Pakistan. There is no safety of life; nobody knows when a bomb would explode in the middle of the road and kill innocent bystanders. The government has lost control of the law and order situation in the country. The middle and upper class is afraid of the poor and religiously rigid lower section of the society. The jihadists and Talibanis do not want to see any influence of the west prevailing in their country. In a way the normal social and cultural activities are heavily influenced by these old conservative preachers called Mullahs. And people are afraid that if they go against Mullah's preaching they could be putting their lives in danger.

The population of Pakistan is exploding; it is 189 million strong at this time-year 2013. There is no birth control in the country and polygamy is legal and in fashion. There are absolutely no rights for a Muslim woman; her status is above slavery. A Muslim man is the king of the kingdom. At the top of all this upheaval, the politicians and the government employees are deeply involved in corruption practices. The resultant affect is chaos and instability in the country. In addition, the neighboring country, Afghanistan is full of anti-American militants who want to enforce strict Muslim laws which prohibit any kind of freedom to Muslim woman including education. The whole environment is toxic and it will take a strong government in Pakistan to make the country a safe and desirable place to live. The odds are heavy.

Arts and cultural activities flourish when there is peace and an environment for creativity and freedom of action is present; when the element of fear is present, there could not be any progress in terms of expression of thoughts and social interactions. Pakistan is passing through a critical phase in its history and drastic steps are needed badly to change the present situation. The coming five years could move the country in the right direction and once again the people of Pakistan can move forward with hope and happiness. All of us look for a better future for ourselves and for the next generation. Pakistani people are not different.

The present conditions in the country are not conducive to openness and acceptance of American style interactions, socially and culturally mainly because there is fear of reprisal leading up to kidnapping and even murder. The middle class of Pakistan has become more religious and anti-U.S.A and western way of life. In other words, it has closed its door to modern society. Gradually when the economic conditions of the country improve, there would be more receptiveness and acceptance of different avenues of thoughts and greater interactions within and outside the country. When the people are engaged in bread and butter questions only, how could anybody, expect a momentum in social and cultural fields. Indian movies are banned in Pakistan and only Muslim culture is admired. It is hoped that Pakistan would not follow the path of Iran and there would be more interactions socially and culturally within the country and with outside world. The next five years are crucial in this direction. Religious bigotry and oppressive poverty are the main reasons that are turning many Pakistani to become terrorists and suicide bombers. Illiteracy and high unemployment are other reasons that are changing the everyday life of a Pakistani citizen.

There are some similarities between Hindu culture of India and Muslim culture of Pakistan. Music, arts and crafts, food, way of living, dresses and socially acceptable norms and traditions have common roots. The big difference comes from religion and it is a big dividing line. Both countries are fanatic about Cricket and love hot and spiced food. Interestingly, Indian and Pakistani nationals look so similar; it is difficult to distinguish them.

The next five years in Pakistan's social and cultural arena would depend upon economic conditions and peace and stability in the country. If the Islamic militants are not controlled, if the religious clerics are not warned about their teachings of hatred and intolerance for other communities and finally if rampant corruption is not eliminated, Pakistan would be facing enormous difficulties and that is bound to affect the cultural and social life of its citizens.

It is a fact that Pakistani nationals who are living in England, and the United States have a tremendous influence in changing the cultural and social values of local Pakistani society; that is needed.

.

Japan

Japan: The highly industrialized country of Asia and the third largest economy of the world are moving to new directions in 2013; the political scenario is changing fast. Gone are those days when Japan could dictate its wishes to China, Korea and other Asian countries. China has transformed itself into a global world power and Japan has receded into a second class military power with very little influence in global military conflicts. The new Chinese government has told repeatedly that all the small islands lying within South China Seas belonged to China and no other country including Japan, Philippines, Viet Nam and Malaysia has any legitimate claims on these. Japan is furious; so are other Asian countries especially Philippines and Viet Nam.

Realizing the new stature of China, Japan is looking for strengthening its military relations with Australia, India and the United States. This hostility brewing between Japan and China is causing concern in political circles. United States has already made its position known by declaring that these islands are disputed territories and China cannot claim them as its own.

The newly elected Prime Minister of Japan Mr. Shinto Abe is leaning towards the idea that Japan should abandon the idea of keeping Japan as a non military power. He is in favor of reviving Japanese Navy, Air force and ground military battalions. Japan has the capabilities to become once again a great military power but the world has to evaluate the consequences of it. We do not want to see another General Tojo in Japan. We want to see Japan as a great economic power but we can not see Japan rising again as a great military power. It is a scary feeling.

The old military victories of Japan would not let it go down under the new rising Chinese tides of strength and influence. Both countries have to compromise on their rigid positions; that is the only solution for those islands. This situation has prompted Japan to forge closer military ties with Australia and India. Is this trend going for a short period of time or for a long term? That has to be seen. One thing is for sure, Japan and China may exert their national pride to influence other countries of Pacific Asia. Most probably, countries like India and Indonesia are going to side with Japan rather with China. We must however, not forget that global politics is never a stagnant pool; new waves emerge quite often.

What changes are we going to see in Japan in the next five years in terms of Social and Cultural trends? The last twenty years in Japanese history point out in one definite direction and that is pro-western. The new Japan is a carbon copy of any western European state, with certain exceptions. Shinto, Buddhist and Christian religions would continue to guide the daily life of an average Japanese citizen. Fast food, western dress, democratic values and technological advances have become the norms in Japanese culture. There are some historical conditioning of attitudes of Japanese towards Chinese, Koreans and other Pacific Asians which prevent them to integrate more closely. Things are changing, however. It has been reported that many Japanese young men are getting married to Philippine girls.

During World War II, Japanese community living in the United States had to undergo many hardships which were unjust and discriminatory. But those days have gone by and better relations have been built between American and local Japanese citizens; Japanese American community is playing an important role in the American social and cultural activities. Among Asian American citizens, Indians, Chinese and Japanese pay highest attention to education and no wonder they are very well placed in the society stratum. It is difficult to point out what the land of the rising sun, that is Japan, would be introducing to cultural and social arena in the next five years, in its own country or outside.

When we look at Japan, we have to look at the country from the perspectives of Eastern versus Western philosophical, cultural and social values, norms and traditions. Though the world is getting flat and becoming more inclusive and cohesive in nature, yet certain subtle differences would remain in tact between the people of these two hemispheres. At this juncture it is the East that is adopting more and more of the Western way of life with some local adjustments and variations and at the same token more western countries and its citizens have started appreciating Eastern values and its culture. There is a good melting pot.

The next five years in Japanese Cultural and Social scene do not indicate any radical changes from the existing one. Like any other thing in this world, subtle changes are bound to take place.

Soviet Russia

Russia: The largest country in the world, Russia formally known as United Soviet Socialist Republics before its break up in 1991, has become a non Communist country now. By all standards, it is relatively a poor country with a Gross National Income of $10.6 K per capita. The average National Income of a Western European Country is $39K. It is a great nuclear power and one of the largest exporting countries of military equipment especially to China, India and other Asian and Middle East countries. It has a large reservoir of Gas and Oil; it is the largest supplier of Gas to the European countries and the largest producer of Vodka. Russia was the first country to send the man across the globe but failed to land on the Moon surface. Only the United States has the distinction of achieving this remarkable feat. Lenin wanted to change the conditions of poverty and deprivation of the Russian citizens but unfortunately the average Russian at this point in time does not belong to a well to do society. Rocket Science, Nuclear Arms and Equipment, Oil and Gas are in abundance in Russia but basic manufacturing facilities are missing commodities in the country.

Russia has declared itself as a non Communist country but it has failed to make any significant headway in transforming itself from the communistic way of governing the country to a western style democratic set up. Corruption, autocratic ways of doing things, incompetence and lack of business dexterity are the hall marks of Russian government. Compared to Russia, China has done a wonderful job in transforming itself from a rural, agricultural country to become the manufacturing workshop of the globe.

The country is well known for ice skating, ice hockey and ballet dancing. Novels, Stories and Poems written by Russian authors have been translated into other languages and they are considered great piece of literature. Russians have bagged many gold medals in Olympic Games. The country is witnessing many encouraging signs of freedom of expression and political opposition. Days of Stalin brutality and torture have been officially banished from the Russian society. However, there are very few structural changes towards a more democratic set up. The old ways of doing things still persist in the society. It seems that Russia would take more time before it could compare itself with other western countries.

A radical change from Communism to a non Communistic government structure is not an easy make over. It will take a long time for Russians to adjust their life style forced upon them by changes in government structure, society adjustments and external factors. Many countries which were once, part of the United Soviet Socialist Republic, became independent countries in 1990-1991 and the whole political make up of the country changed; people were not fully prepared for all these changes. President Gorbachev was instrumental for introducing history making changes in the lives of Russians and the history of Russian Republic. A new chapter was written in the global political, social and cultural scene by the changes that took place in U.S.S.R

Stalin ruled over Russia as a ruthless dictator; millions were tortured to death. However, he transformed Russia to a military

Super Power. Under Communism, there was no individual freedom; cultural and social life was dictated by the Communist elites. Russians were making good progress in sports arena, ballet dancing, ice skating and various athletic activities were promoted by the Communist government and every thing was controlled and run by the Communist System. It must be noted that Cultural and Social advancements in any society is governed by the most important factor of freedom of expression, freedom of action and absence of poverty. Nothing thrives in gloomy and dark clouds of hunger and famine. Russia was a far cry from abundance after World War II. Cultural and Social events were not in the lime light. Western European governments got help from the United States but Russia had to stand on its own feet.

What is in store for Russia in the next five years, politically, culturally and socially? The answer is: there is no limit. We see myriad of all kinds of changes that can take place in the Russian society. It has to catch up a lot in many areas, with the rest of the world, especially with the western countries of Europe. The standard of living for an average Russian is very low compared to a western European and it will take some time for it to make up the lost time. The question is whether Russian leadership is competent and capable of transforming their country to a level which may be comparable to European or American standards. It is tough.

Germany

Germany: The largest economy of Europe with a Gross Domestic Product exceeding three trillions dollar, is brimming with prosperity and lowest unemployment rates. Everybody in Europe thinks that it is Germany that could save the collapsing economies of Greece, Spain, Portugal and other similarly placed countries where the unemployment rates are soaring and people are very much frustrated over the economic conditions. It has been reported that one in four young men and women, living in those countries, is out of job. To remedy this problem, the European Union is allocating six billion Euros to provide training to the unemployed. The conditions are bad and it will take many hard decisions to take, to solve this problem.

The rise and fall of Hitler made the country go through many traumatic experiences. The division into East and West Germany and finally the unification has transformed the country and at this point, it is one of the largest exporters in the world. Autos, Chemicals, Heavy machines and other products are the leading exported items of Germany. They are well known for their quality and reliability. As long as the global economy keeps on chugging along in the right direction, the German economy will continue to grow and more and more jobs would be created. The environment for business expansion is well entrenched in the German culture. There is a consensus between employers and workers about working conditions and there is no dearth of skilled workforce.

Germany is famous for its Composers, Philosophers and Men of Literature. Germany along with France has laid the foundation of European Union and right now is the major provider of financial assistance to the weaker economies of its members. The question many people in Germany are asking why should we bail out those countries which are not capable of governing themselves in prudent manner? Countries, where jobs are not created proportionately to their needs, would more than often, run into these situations and it would be difficult to lift them up. It is the government, its people and the business environment which is responsible for creating the right conditions for countries to grow and make economic progress. Stagnation and frustration would be the result for not being efficient and competitive.

Very recently, the German Chancellor Angela Merkel stated that Germany needs 200,000 Engineers. Naturally, these positions would be filled by nationals from Germany, Greece, Spain,

Portugal, Turkey and other Eastern European countries. That means a significant intermingling of different cultures. Just as in the United States, it is bound to have important repercussion in the society when people from different countries live and work together. As long as Neo Nazis are kept under surveillance, German society would be enriched by this work experience. Germans are hard and smart working people and this opportunity could be utilized to show to other countries that Germans could be helpful and friendly to others when they are needed. The old history of Germany has to be rewritten.

The past history of Germany has antagonized many countries and lot of people but people change, country change and change is the name of the game. The next five years in Germany's cultural and social life would hinge upon its own attitude towards the people of other countries that would be living in Germany and working there on a temporary basis. There are exceptionally very few countries in the world where intermingling of different cultures and way of life could be integrated with out facing lot of problems; the society norms and traditions do come in the way and they create all kinds of hindrance and troubles. German society has to open its door of understanding and give and take attitude in order to make this phenomenon a success.

No body wants to see Germany becoming a military power and very few would like to see it dictating the policies of other countries; the present economic conditions in Europe are presenting such kind of situations. Germany should not overstep the boundary lines of interference in other countries governing policies. Socially, it could create serious problems.

Germany has placed itself in a very enviable position; its economic growth would propel its society to move in many diverse directions and subsequently will create for itself greater achievements, culturally and socially. As long as the goals are clearly laid out, German influence would move forward.

Australia

Australia: One of the most prosperous countries of the world, Australia with a small population of only twenty two million people is voted as a safe and most desirable place to live. It has more than ninety percent Caucasian population, mostly from England and Ireland. A country which is as big as the United States has lot of potentials to become a Super Power provided correct and aggressive policies on immigration are put in place. It will require bold Vision and clear cut goals and objectives. The United States of America stands today on the highest pedestal because the immigrants placed it on that position. Countries like Australia and Canada have this great opportunity to follow this proven path. Cautious leadership and status quo mentality would prevent it to move in that direction.

Australia is not England, France or Italy where regional customs and traditions have taken deep roots in the society; in fact it is a country which can not boast of a golden history of its own. However, it is a newly discovered land of great opportunities and it can carve out its future to unlimited potentials. Till very recently, Australia was following "White Only" policies similar to South Africa but now the situation has changed. The Australian government openly affirms now that Australians are not racists; however, there are certain rogue elements in the society that persist in following their own agenda and give hard time to Asians especially to Indians. Looking broadly, it seems that integration between local Australians and Asians will take a long time. If we want to see conditions similar to the United States where Asians have established themselves very well, the local Australian community has to make concerted efforts to welcome the Asian members. Genuine feelings of appreciation of Asian culture would make the difference. This transformation of attitude towards

Asians would definitely help Australia move towards greater growth and prosperity. Contribution from Asian immigrants could be very significant.

During the last ten years (2003-13), the Australian society has seen some changes in terms of interactions and intermingling with others and the Australian leaders have started feeling that they are surrounded by Asian countries and they have to become a part of this phenomenon. In order to prosper, they have to trade with Asian countries more than with Europeans and Americans. In the long run, this introspection would lead to better relations between these two continents. It is the younger generation which is outlining the future of our world and in this new world as to speak, there is no place for arrogance and racial superiority; it is the knowledge and expertise which would dictate the conditions and environments in which we would be living. The world would be more flat than ever before.

The Australian government has to face the problem of asylum seekers who are interested in settling down in Australia. The core problem which is the driving force for people to seek asylum in other countries is connected with poverty and lack of opportunities in their own countries. Australia offers a good environment for living a comfortable life; that attracts people of various countries especially Indonesians, Bangladeshi, Iraqi and others. Most of these people are unskilled and can become a source of burden to the state. No wonder, the Australian government hesitates to take any big step. It is unfortunate that our world is exploding in population and the resources are dwindling with the result that poverty and deprivation is increasing; the global leadership has failed to tackle this situation which could become a big tragedy.

What changes we could expect, politically, economically, socially and culturally in Australian society in the next five years, are not very difficult to project. Unless the Australian leadership makes a drastic turn to inefficiency, corruption, wrong financial and economic policies which seems rather remote possibilities, we see a bright future for the country in the horizon. The chances of hitting recession are not visible at this time; the social and cultural environment of the Australian society would move forward with more interactions and influence from outside sources. If China takes some wrong steps in its foreign policy, it will have some consequential momentum in realignment of Australia with the United States and most probably with Japan and India, too.

United States and United Kingdom have become the converging centers in the world, culturally and socially; we see the same pattern for Canada and may be for Australia, too.

France

France: The Socialist candidate Hollande defeated the incumbent President Sarkozy in the election of 2012. After two years in the office, his popular ratings have plummeted because he could not deliver what he had promised. The unemployment figure is still very high and he could not raise the taxes on the rich community because of the strong opposition. He did not hire 30,000 teachers as he had promised and the budget deficit remained high. France public spending per capita is still the highest in the Eurozone. At the top of all this France is facing zero growth in economy. The financial rating of the country has been downgraded from AAA to a lower AA. President Hollande has also run into a personal love story affair with an actress which does not augers well for him.

With this background, we have to look what kind of dynamism we could expect from the second largest economy of Europe? The austerity program of the Socialist Party is not popular with the general public and no body wants a reduction of the governments public spending. With high unemployment and zero growth, recession is bound to prevail for a longer period of time. Under these conditions, France has to renegotiate with the European

Union, the financial burden it has to entail to support the weaker economies of Europe like Greece and Spain, in order to put its own house on financial stability. Some economic gurus are predicting that England will replace France as the second largest economy of Europe in a decade or so. If things do not change drastically very soon, chances are that France may lose its second position in the European community.

Let us look into some personal relationship bonds between the top executives of France, Germany, England and the United States. President Sarkozy had built a cozy relationship with President Bush. He and his wife stayed in Buckingham Palace as a personal guest of Queen Elizabeth which shows he had a good rapport with the British government. And then, he and German Chancellor Angela Markel had established close working relationship between the two of them. That shows that President Sarkozy was keen on building a close knit circle of political friendship for the good of France and for the rest of the world. It is without any doubt that personal relationship between the heads of the states is of paramount importance in the present day world. Many crisis can be resolved if there is trust and friendship among the top leaders. Not to down play President Hollande, it has been reported that he is rather modest and has a quite personality and does not prefer loud showmanship. He has his own personality and there is nothing wrong about it. President Hollande will continue to have friendly and cordial relations with the United States, England and Germany. He may not be able to enforce higher taxes on the rich people and might be forced to cut down public spending. In Feb 2014, President Hollande made an official visit to the United States; President Obama and President Hollande stated that the United States and France are enjoying the closest relationship and there are no outstanding issues between the two countries.

The world's economy is slowly coming out of recession and that would help the French economy as well. When the political situation improves in the Arabic world, it will have a positive impact on its economy. France is a big military hardware supplier-fighter airplanes, nuclear submarines and fast moving tanks-are exported through out the world. Airbus, the second largest manufacturer of commercial planes in the world is located in France. French speaking Algeria, Tunisia, Morocco and other African countries have strong business ties with France and that is bound to have a very positive impact on the French economy in the long run. President Hollande is trying to push business dealings with China, India and South Korea. If he succeeds in his efforts, he will turn around the economy of France in a big way.

It is said Paris is the throbbing heart of every young lover; indeed it is a beautiful city with lot of good wine and variety of cheeses to satisfy our culinary taste. Tourist industry is a big foreign exchange earner. People from all corners of the world want to see Paris and enjoy its beauty. Designer clothes and beauty products from France are welcomed all over the world. Liberty, Equality and Fraternity were first coined in France. It is a true democratic country and we hope it will continue to be that way.

Where France would be in five years

We are trying to project an image of France extended to twenty, twenty (2020). Under President Hollande, if the global economy takes the turn for the better and if he proves himself as a good salesman, building solid business connections with countries like China, India and other emerging countries, the economy would lift off and the present conditions would change. He has to be aggressive in his moves and sharp in negotiations otherwise he would fail in his mission. The worst scenario would be if the growth rate does not move appreciably and unemployment remains high. In that situation the government would have to renegotiate its commitment to European Union. Defense industry, Aerospace and nuclear related items would be able to pull out the country from its present doldrums. Private enterprise as well as the government's earnest efforts would be the key factor in this equation. An optimistic picture of all this analysis is that tourists would continue to flood Paris gates; French wine cellars would be flowing in bounty and delicious packages of cheese would be sold in abundance whatever may be the projections of this study.

Italy

Italy: It is a country where art and culture have created beautiful cities of Rome, Florence and Venice; needless to say, Italy is a very popular tourist destination. It is also the home of the Pope, located in the city of Vatican. Rome is full of magnificent churches and remarkable historical monuments. However, with all its past glories, the present picture is not rosy; the country is under tremendous pressure to lift itself from deep recession, negative growth and very high unemployment rate. The public debt is around 120% of Gross Domestic Product and it has to borrow money from European Union to run the government.

The fourth largest economy of Europe with a gross national income of $36 k per capita is famous for its Designer clothes and dresses like Ralph Polo, Sports Cars, Pasta and variety of wines. It is also associated with Mafia gangs and rampant corruption prevailing all over the government agencies, politicians and business people. There is no stability in the governing bodies.

It has been reported that the central government of Italy has changed hands, at least ten times, after World War II. It is just pathetic to note that politicians and business community has been manipulating the common man and pocketing all the gains in their favor and the country is going down the hill. The richest man of Italy and two times Prime Minister, Mr. Silvio Berlusconi had been running the show for almost two decades. In 2013, however, he was expelled from the Senate and has been charged with tax evasion, fraud and having sex with a teenager. It is a shame that people like him were not banned for life at the very beginning; the Italian people should have thrown him out long time ago. He has brought disgrace to the country.

The country needs a dynamic leader who can straighten out the filth and dirt of the present Italian politics; a person of uncorrupt distinction, a man of vision and a doer; not afraid of Maffia gangsters and should be experienced and sharp in running the government. Only then, Italy will come out of its present economic crisis. Borrowing money or tightening belt on expenditure would not solve the problem. Italy needs a radical reform in its governing structure; it needs growth; expansion in trade and commerce. It is in the hands of the young generation to throw out corrupt officials and business guards and replace them with those people who care for the ordinary citizens. It is tough but it could be done.

Interestingly, the Mayor of Florence, Mr.Renzi has emerged as a young charismatic leader, of the Democratic Party PD who openly says that Italian politics has to change and new ideas have to be brought in the governing system. If he succeeds in his bid to be the next Prime-Minister of Italy, it seems very likely that the country would see better days ahead. Note: Mr.Renzi has become the Prime Minister of Italy. The older generation of Italian politicians has failed to rise to the occasion and the country is facing the harsh realities of very high unemployment and stagnant economic growth. The existing vicious environment of corruption has to be eliminated altogether; there should not be any excuses for its continuation. It is true for any country; corruption corrodes.

Let us examine the future prospects of Italy in the next five years or so. It could be said without hesitation that the country needs drastic measures to come out of the present dismal situation. In our prognosis, it will be a fresh, smart and competent leadership that would save the country from further erosion. Austerity measures and pinching big business would not be able to take the country for a long haul. Italian textile industry as well as the auto industry along with thriving tourist bonanza will keep the country chugging along but the drastic measures would have to be placed in proper places for the country to move forward in the real sense. There is no reason for Italy to become a drag in the European Union; it has all the potentials for greater prosperity.

Turkey

Turkey: Kemal Ataturk founded the Republic of Turkey in 1920 after the disintegration of Ottoman Empire. It is a country where people of different religions could live in peace and harmony unlike many other Muslim countries like Pakistan and Afghanistan. Kemal had made a point to keep religion separate from the State and secularism was enshrined in the constitution. It is a moderate Muslim country and the general public is not crazy about the religion. The military wielded a powerful influence in running the government and considered its responsibility to keep the country a secular state. The present government is headed by President Gul and Prime Minister Erdogan representing Justice and Development Party called AKP. This is an Islamic Party but it emphasizes that it is not going to bring in Islamic agenda like Sharia laws. However, wearing a head scarf is now legal which the military had opposed in the past. At the same time, it seems that the influence of the Army is gradually fading away.

Istanbul previously called Constantinople, capital city of Byzantine Empire has a mixture of Muslim and Christian make up in terms of its culture and architecture. It is a great tourist attraction and is the opening door way to the Black Sea. This tiny portion of the country is located in the European continent and carries more of the European flavor than Asian. Turkey in the past had good relations with Israel but recently Prime Minister Erdogan has publicly denounced Israel over the issue of Palestine refugees and the friendly bash has disappeared.

Turkey has been trying to become a member of the European Union for more than a decade but solid opposition from France and Germany and other countries have denied this opportunity to the country. They are offering Privileged membership but not the regular one. If the present conditions prevail, Turkey would not be able to become a full fledged member of the European Union. It is a member of NATO and has a strong army to support its international role. In fact, it is trying to play an important role in Afghanistan and many Muslim countries feel that Turkey is a good role model to follow. Pakistan leadership is eagerly seeking to follow Turkish government model. Looking from economic point of view, Turkey is doing alright- not very spectacular growth but not bad at all. The per capita income is $10K; the population is 75 million strong and the country is stable.

In 2014, Prime Minister Erdogran had been under pressure to resign; many institutions especially Judiciary Branch has taken a lead to force resignations of many influential central government ministers on charges of corruption. However, AKP is still the main political force and the Army is keeping away from intervention. Under these conditions, Mr.Erdogran will continue to be in charge. Turkey has a small minority of Kurdish people who had been fighting for an independent state. Iraq also has a Kurdish populated area and they too want to be independent. Down the road, Kurdish people might carve out an independent country of their own, if the conditions are favorable. Saddam Hussain had killed thousands of innocent Kurdish civilians when he was President of Iraq.

Let us put together some important features of the Turkish landscape which would dictate the future course of action that the country will take in the next five years or so. Turkey might accept the Privileged Membership of the European Union, as a last resort. It will help the country in many ways, especially in terms of foreign direct investment and a bigger slice of export to the European countries. It will also mean enforcing more democratic practices in governing the country as well as in planting these values in many important sectors of the society like freedom of the press and freedom of speech. Some of these attributes are missing in the present set up of the Turkish society and that is not right.

As we see it today, Turkey will move along with steady progress in terms of economic growth and more democratic system of the government, more freedom of speech and perhaps more religious leaning of the government towards Islamic culture. It is also looking apparent that the Army is not inclined to interfere in the government affairs. The present Turkish leadership of President Gul and Prime-Minster Erdogan, which is running the government for almost a decade, is interested in assuming leadership role in the Muslim world especially in emerging countries like Pakistan, Afghanistan and Indonesia. It has taken a strong pro-Palestinian stand and is supporting the rebels against President Assad in Syria. As long as the Turkish government maintains a secular status and keep the religious fervor at bay, it will be good for the country as well as good for the global community.

Brazil

Brazil: The largest country of South America is Brazil-it is as big as the United States. The population is around 200 millions and Gross National Income is eleven thousand dollars per capita. It is self sufficient in oil and has a large deposit of iron ore. It is a country of very rich and poor-a big gap between the two sections. In the recent past, it has seen booms and busts in its economy. At present, Brazil is going ahead with stable currency and economic progress. Like many other emerging countries, it has lot of corruption prevailing in the government institutions. It is a country of mixed races-Portuguese, Africans, local Indians and mixture of different communities.

The present government is headed by Ms Dilma Rousseff. She was chief Assistant of President Lula da Silva, a very popular and successful leader of Brazil. One of the largest democracies of the world, Brazil enjoys personal freedom of speech and it has established an environment for free press, a big difference when we compare Brazil with other South American countries, where dictatorship had been a normal form of the government. It has been reported that the Brazilian economy has taken over the British economy which is ranked number six in the world, with a Gross Domestic Product exceeding 2.4 trillion dollars. Brazil has the largest army, navy and Air force in South America. Because of its present economic strength, Brazil has taken the top position among the South American countries. It is not a pro-Russia or pro U.S country-it is a country where the national interest counts the most. It is not a Non Aligned nation. The leadership of Brazil is engrossed in improving the conditions of millions of people who have no land, no jobs and no house to live. Because of the large gap between the rich land owners and landless farmers and jobless workers, the Brazilian government is facing tough times. Unless and until the land redistribution takes place, the country would continue to have difficulties in terms of social unrest, political upheaval and riots. In the largest cities of Brazil, Sao Paulo and Rio de Janeiro, one third of the population lives in slums called Falevas. It is a matter of shame that a small minority of people lives in huge palatial houses. The government should take some drastic measures to redistribute this wealth, more evenly.

Brazil is the largest producer of Coffee and Ethanol and very recently it has discovered large amount of off shore oil reserves; it has plenty of iron ore, too. However, with all these pluses, the country has many negatives. The corruption is very common and there is no transparency in government dealings. The country lacks skilled managers; there are no prestigious educational institutions and the infrastructure is in bad shape. Looking from these perspectives, it seems likely that Brazil will move along with a moderate economic growth in the near future but the long term prospects look promising.

With the advent of new emerging industrial countries-China, India and Brazil-the global economical and political map is being redrawn. Eight highly industrialized countries of the globe called G 8 have recognized the role of other emerging countries and have been transformed into Group of 20, led by China, India and Brazil. There is no difference of opinion among industrialized countries to recognize the importance of the up coming developing countries. The planet is going to be moved forward not by the developed countries alone any more –the developing countries would also be the active partners in this endeavor. The world will hear many voices especially from developing countries in the coming decades. Brazil as it seems now, will take its prominent position in the global economic and political set up, very soon.

The 1916 Summer Olympic Games are going to be staged in Rio de Janeiro; it is a great historic moment for Brazil and it is the first Olympic game to be held in South America. That means lot of expenditure for building new stadiums and improving infrastructure to handle the flow of thousands of spectators for the game. President Rousseff is known as an iron lady and is determined to root out corruption from the government agencies; however she has to manage the finances. The country is not receiving the oil revenues at present from new reserves; it will take few years to materialize the hefty cash flow, so increase in commodity exports like Coffee, Iron ore and Sugar is the other viable alternative. Looking from a broad perspective, the country needs good education system, sharp and competent business managers, improvement in economic conditions for the masses and eradication of corrupt practices in the society at large.

The other important countries of South America are Argentina, Chile, Venezuela, Columbia and Peru. Argentina may come up fast, in terms of influence with other neighborly countries. Venezuela on the other hand, is trying to spread Communist, Socialist ideology among the South American countries using its oil resources as a powerful media. However, it is Brazil that stands out as the most important country that could represent the South American Continent. There is no doubt that along with China and India, Brazil will become a powerful voice in shaping the future trends of global inter relationship. It has all the potentials to be a great country but it will require strong leadership. When we write about Brazil, we have to mention the name of Lula da Silva, a remarkable man. He rose from no where; belonged to a very poor family, started his career as a shoe shine boy on the street and started the Movement of Landless Rural Workers and finally got the crown, the Presidency of Brazil. He moved millions of landless farmers and unemployed Brazilians out of abject poverty.

Mexico

Mexico: The second largest economy of Latin America, Mexico has very good potentials to move towards prosperity and higher standard of living because it has oil and gas and is a member of North America Free Trade Association which opens up a big door for exports to the United States and Canada. It is a democratic country, has free press and freedom of speech. After the economic crisis of 2008 when the United States ran into problems, Mexico gradually came out of it and in 2010 it attracted a good chunk of foreign direct investment that stabilized the economy and the picture started looking good.

The unfortunate part of Mexico is that it has become the haven for drug smuggling and consequently kidnapping and day time murders have become the norm of the society. There is a big divide between the rich Spanish and the poor indigenous population. The country has been run by Institutional Revolution Party called PRI for more than seventy years; the present President of Mexico Enrique Pena Nieto also belongs to PRI. He won the election in 2012 and has promised to eliminate the small local drug lords and root out corruption and bring peace and stability in the country. How far can he succeed, has to be seen.

President Bush in 2006 ordered to build a 3000 kilometer long border wall to stop illegal migration to the United States. At one point in time, more than a million people per year were trying to cross over to the United States. It is estimated that at present there are ten million Mexican citizens who are living in the United States illegally. There are big debates between Democrats and Republicans to solve this problem of so called illegal Mexican migrants. Democrats are leaning towards granting U.S citizenship to these people who are already living in the States and paying taxes but Republicans have certain reservations.

In this twenty first century, if the country is plagued by lack of governing efficiency and on top, grounded in rampant corruption from the highest to the bottom of the society, there are very remote chances, that it will make any head way towards steady progress. Mexico has to transform its social and economic structure by building an environment of safety, hope and fair distribution of national wealth to the poor people who have no choice but to cross.

When Mexico became the member of NAFTA, it was hoped that it will have the advantage of capturing large export markets of U.S.A and Canada but it did not materialize. China, a far distant country with a similar production cost scenario became the number one supplier and Mexico remained behind. The bottom line in all business dealings falls on quality, price and delivery which China did very well. The customer in the United States and Canada has no hesitation in buying products made in China but that is not true in case of Mexico. The country has to improve its productivity and efficiency standards in order to compete against the best. It means establishing good education institutions as well as providing affordable, health programs to the common man and woman of the country; they go hand in hand.

It is an irony that Mexico has to face many formidable problems at the same time. Eradicating drug business which amounts almost to thirteen billions yearly, lifting the poor from dire poverty, building new infrastructure to support business, establishing high caliber education institutions and keep up the oil and gas production and at the same time banish corruption, all these tasks are not easy. It will require a strong commitment and bold leadership. Many of the Latin American as well as emerging developing countries are facing similar tough situations. All these countries have to move with Vision, dedication and determination to achieve their goals. The other alternative is slow progress or even stagnation, inflation and recession.

When we sum up the major factors which have to be in proper places in order to move the country forward, we conclude that Mexico will make progress but spectacular results will not be achieved in the near future. The war on smuggling will take a long time; even with the help of the United States, the drug lords will be difficult to eliminate and the country will continue to face murders and kidnapping. The second major task for Mexican government will be how to pull out millions of poor people out of unemployment and dire poverty. Large foreign investment and intelligent financial management will be the most important instrument to achieve higher economic growth and steady progress. It is a stupendous task, no doubt but Mexico needs it.

Indonesia

Indonesia: After two hundred years of Dutch rule, Indonesia got its independence in 1949 under the leadership of President Soekarno, a charismatic freedom fighter. A country of thousand islands and huge ethnic diversity, it is the largest Muslim country with a population of 250 million strong and a Gross National Income of $4k per capita. In 1965, Communist Party of Indonesia staged a coup to topple President Soekarno but it failed; six army generals were murdered and after the coup, thousands of people, most of them were Chinese Indonesians were killed by the army. General Suharto became the chief Army Commander and in 1967 Sukarno resigned and handed over the Presidency to Suharto. He transformed an agricultural country into a modern industrialized nation. Under his authoritarian military rule, Indonesia made good progress but at the same time, corruption also spread throughout. He stayed in power for more than three decades; he was forced out in 1998 and after few years, Soekarno's daughter, Sukarnoputri became the President. She did not prove to be a strong President and in 2004 elections General Susilo Yudhoyona defeated her and he is the present President of Indonesia after getting reelected in 2009. He is a popular leader but corruption and lack of efficient governing structure are holding the country behind.

Political and economical alliances: Indonesia is an active member of ASEAN-Association of South East Asian Nations, OPEC, ICO (Islamic Countries Organization) as well as Non Aligned Nations. In 2009, Secretary of State, Hillary Clinton signed a Comprehensive Partnership Treaty under U.S Foreign Aid Program which would provide technical and monetary assistance in improving Health, Education and Agricultural production. President Obama visited Indonesia in 2010 and he reaffirmed his commitment to provide necessary help in raising the economic growth of Indonesia. The country suffered a serious jolt in 2004, when an underground earthquake rattled the island of Sumatra taking away more than 200,000 lives and sending tsunami waves to Thailand, India and Ceylon causing heavy damage to property and thousand of lives were lost. On this occasion, the whole world came together. This was the moment when people from all walks of life realized the pain and anguish of this terrible natural disaster.

Looking from the strategic point of view, Indonesia along with India, Australia and Japan can form a powerful alliance with the United States to counter the influence of China and Russia in Asia. It is a very certain assumption that China will be coming very close to challenge the supremacy of the United States in South and Pacific Asia in not too distant future, and it is imperative for the United States to start looking for future partners to face this impending danger in the Asian peninsula. We can add South Korea and Thailand in this block to resist the advance of aggressive China and the cold war proponent Russia.

When the global economy was going strong, Indonesia had registered a growth of 5% in its Gross Domestic Product. In 2008, the U.S economy was going hay wire and it had rippling effect all over the world. However, most of the Asian countries were not too much affected by this down turn; it did have some repercussion though. Indonesian economy slowed down but it picked up slowly. Indonesia has oil and gas, palm oil and rubber and now has become a big exporter of textile, wooden products and spices. If the country could get rid of corruption which has embroiled the whole society, provide good infrastructure to business and set up a professional group of business executives to oversee the functions of the governing institutions, the country would be able to achieve quantum leaps in efficiency and national growth. If these factors are not put in place, Indonesia will move forward marginally or may even slip down in the next five years or so.

Indonesia is a moderate Muslim country; one of its famous islands, Bali is still a Hindu state and there are many Buddhists temples located in the main island of Java where Buddhism flourished around eight century. However, Al Qaeda and their followers did penetrate into Indonesia and in 2002 more than two hundred people died, mostly Australians in a bomb explosion that was planted in a hotel in Bali. The majority of Indonesian people condemned it and it seems very likely that Indonesia would not support anti U.S or anti western ideology and secularism would prevail in the country. It is a reality that poverty and religious bigotry has common language; Indonesian people are smart enough to distinguish between the right and the wrong.

Malaysia

Malaysia: A country of thirty million strong with a Gross National Income of $13K per capita per year is endowed with oil and gas, palm oil, rubber, tin and timber; it is the largest manufacturer of computer disc drives and exporter of textile, steel and autos. It can also boast of one of the tallest buildings in the world called Petronas Towers. It is populated with three distinct communities- 60% are local Muslim Malaysians, 25% are Chinese and 15% are Indians. The Chinese community is the richest whereas the Indian population sits at the bottom and Bhumiputras, the local Malaysians occupy the government corridors. That is how the country is divided. It has a diverse culture of Islam, Hindus, Buddhists and Tao followers. The country got its independence from Britain in 1957 and is a member of the Commonwealth.

In 1969, the local Malaysian community staged an anti Chinese demonstration and demanded better economic and political opportunities for them. That prompted the government to introduce minimum quota system in business, government and civil services for native Malaysians. Ten years later, Dr Mahathir Mohamad, a physician by profession and leader of United Malays National Organization became the Prime Minister of Malaysia. He was an authoritarian but practical leader as well as anti west and pro Islam. He governed the country with dedication and transformed Malaysia to a roaring industrial tiger of South East Asia. After twenty two years of his no nonsense administration, he retired in 2003. Mr. Badawi became the next Prime-Minister of Malaysia.

Malaysia is a progressive modern country but it is beset with many problems related to human rights, freedom of speech, freedom of the press, Prejudiced Judicial Practices, bogus and unfair electoral system, Censorship, detention without trial and ethnic discrimination. Political corruption in governing bodies is normal and too much of western ideas and practices are not welcome. The present Prime Minister Najib Razak is well aware of these prevailing shortcomings in the governing system and has openly declared that if we do not address the grievances of the Chinese and Indian minorities related to quota system and other practices, the country will not make any noticeable progress. It is apparent that if the government let go its responsibility, it will fail.

The authoritarian and forceful Dr.Mahathir left the opposition parties in shamble. When his own assistant Anwar Ibrahim disagreed with his policies, he was put behind prison on charges of sodomy. Finally 1n 2012, Mr.Ibrahim was freed and his party now has a good chance to challenge National Front Coalition which has ruled Malaysia for almost sixty years. Many Chinese and Indian Malaysians politicians have expressed their support to Mr.Ibrahim. Prime Minister Razak, a British trained Economist and son of the second Prime Minister, knows very well the role played by the Chinese business community. It is reported that Malaysia has already signed a treaty of Free Trade Agreement with China which has expanded the trade relations between the two countries considerably. Singapore and Taiwan, two other Chinese countries along with Indonesia are important trading partners of Malaysia. Interestingly, India incorporated is not in the list. The Indian community has been given a second class citizenship for some reason or the other; however, the government refutes that charges.

Let us project the political and economical conditions of the country in the next five years or so. Malaysia during Dr.Mahathir leadership was strongly anti west which is not the case now. However, even now the Muslim Malaysian community is not very enthusiastic about western culture though strict Sharia laws are not followed in the judicial system but the Islamic sentiments are strong in the society. No body can dare to say anything against the Koran; that would be considered a crime. Malaysia will not join the United States circle nor will it go with Russia. It is very likely that Malaysia will be forging close ties with China, Indonesia and Singapore, economically and politically.

The presence of dynamic Chinese business community in Malaysia has made a very positive impact in the daily lives of the common man. It is very essential to have smart and sharp business leaders so that the country could move forward with the changing times. It is also very important to have strong and dedicated national leaders to react and enact to ongoing global conditions. Transparency in governance is the litmus test for any government. Corruption at the top echelon is the most treacherous route in terms of national disaster. Present Malaysian leaders are on the right track.

South Korea

South Korea: It is a country of 50 million strong with a Gross National Income of $28K per capita. It is the twelve largest economy of the world. It can boast of having some of the most successful companies like Samsung, Hyundai, Kia, L.G, Gold Star and others which have transformed the digital products and services through out the world. Going back to history, South Korea was invaded by Communist North Korea in 1950 and the war ended in 1953, with the line of demarcation between the two countries at 38th Parallel. United States maintains an army contingent of 40.000 military personnel in South Korea to keep North Koreans soldiers out of sight.

The difference between the North and South is just like darkness and Sunshine; South Korea is thriving and the North is starving. In the last fifty years, millions of North Koreans have died of starvation, ill health and poverty. They have also been subjected to mental and physical torture by the founding father of the country Kim II Sung and his son Kim Jong IL; the present ruler is a young man named Kim Jong un and unfortunately he is following the same dictatorial traditions as his father and grand father imposed upon the poor and helpless North Koreans. The irony is that North Korea now has acquired a nuclear status at the expense of thousand of its poor and helpless citizens.

Realizing the plight of the common citizens of North Korea, President Kim Dea Jung of South Korea started a policy of reconciliation called Sunshine Policy in 2000; it enabled families of two countries to meet and South Korea supplied food, fertilizer and other necessary commodities to North Korea as a gesture of goodwill. President Jung was awarded the Nobel Prize for his peace efforts. However, it was hoped that North Korea will give up its nuclear ambitions. But it did not materialize and in 2008, President Lee bak discontinued the program and the North Korean regime started its old rhetoric propaganda against the United States and South Korea. In most of the countries where dictators rule over the disfranchised citizens, only the elite or the favorite group could enjoy the bounties of good life; the rest are at the mercy of the whimsical ideologies and doctrines of the ruler. Nuclear bombs are more important than the common man and woman of the country.

South Korea is very much affected what happens in North Korea and it is very true that without American military support, South Korea would not have been able to achieve economic progress what it has in the past. Since it is a very important factor for South Korea, let us examine what has changed when Kim Jong IL, was running the country and when the new dictator has taken the charge as the supreme leader. In fact, nothing has changed, if we analyze the whole scenario; the economic and political conditions have remained the same-pathetic and unwarranted. There is no freedom and abject poverty is rampant in North Korea. The selected groups are doing alright but the rest of the general public is facing very harsh conditions in day to day life. The new regime wants massive economic aid from the United States and South Korea in exchange for freezing its nuclear program. In the past Pakistan had supplied nuclear technology to North Korea and Iran for sizeable monetary gains but things have changed now. Most of the Middle Eastern Muslim countries have no money to spend on nuclear arms; North Korea has lost a reliable source of foreign exchange to buy food, fertilizer and other essential daily life commodities. In other words the situation has become worse.

The economic transformation that has taken place in South Korea owes its debt to the family owned business houses called Chaebol. Hyundai, Kia, Samsung are the most successful examples. On a sour note, it has to be mentioned that corruption had penetrated deep inside the circle of politicians and business community. The founder of Hyundai was given a jail sentence on charges of tax evasion and fraud. The military dictators were also involved in high corruption cases as well as in violation of human rights. The present President of South Korea Ms Park Chung hee, daughter of ex President General Park apologized in public for the wrong doing of her father and promised to set up a free and democratic governing structure. It will be good for the country to get rid of the old ways of running family business which are riddled with tax evasion, bribery and hidden assets. South Korea has a bright future ahead; with companies like Samsung you could not go wrong in the business world. United States and South Korea along with Japan, Australia and India can make big changes.

.

Thailand

Thailand: Siam, also called the land of the free, is the only Asian country which was never subjugated by any European power in the modern day history. The present ruler, King Bhumibol is the longest ruling monarch in the world; he became the king of Thailand in 1946. A constitutional monarch, he is revered by many and has earned love and affection of his countrymen. Monarchy, Military and Buddhism run the mainstream of Thailand. A country of 70 million strong with a literacy rate of 95%, it is highly popular with tourists; have some of the most beautiful Buddhist temples in the world. Since 1980, it has transformed itself from a poor agricultural country to a thriving modern day industrial economy with a growth rate around 4% and is moving forward steadily. Bangkok, the capital city of Thailand can boast of some of the finest hotels, night clubs and business organizations.

If we look back at the recent political events in the country, we feel that meddling of the army from time to time in the country's affairs is not only undesirable but also harmful. Under the shadow of a powerful army, the political parties can not discharge their functions properly. In 2006, the duly elected Prime Minister Thaksin Shinawatra was dismissed by the military and rewrote a new constitution. These kinds of activities are against the principles of democratic governing system. The army should keep its hands off from running the government's responsibilities.

After the dismissal of Thaksin, the opposition leader, Abhist Vijjajiva became the Prime Minister but he could not survive the onslaught from pro Thaksin supporters. Finally, in the election of 2011,Ms Yingluck Shinawatra, younger sister of Thaksin secured a resounding victory and succeeded as the first lady Prime Minister of Thailand. PPP, the Peoples Party that Shinawatras represent, is popular mainly with farmers and working class community. At this time, Ms Shinawatra is facing lot of turmoil and political chaos created by the followers of the opposition party, led by Mr. Abhist Vijjajiva. It is unfortunate that these two major political parties of the country resort to violent demonstrations. The government machinery is stalled in this process and many innocent people are killed or injured in this ugly situation. If PPP party gets over this, Ms Shinawatra, will be back as Prime Minister again.

Thailand is the largest exporter of rice in the world; Ms Yingluck Shinawatra had started a program which had entitled farmers higher prices for the rice, higher than the world prices. This has led government to default on payment and farmers are not happy. The opposition party alleges that there is lot of corruption going on in this program and the Prime Minister should be sacked. As soon as the election results are made public, the country would know who will be the next Prime Minister. The early indicators favor Shinawatra but it would not be an easy win.

Let us examine critically the socio-economical and political trends in the country keeping in view certain given factors. Number one: Communist party is outlawed in the country; Russian influence is minimal though Chinese minority which is about fifteen percent does have certain leaning towards mainland China. Japan is number one investor in the country; Japanese and Thai monarchies are on friendly terms. Auto, electronics, textiles, and lumber are important export items. Tourist industry is thriving well. The corruption index is not high. The negative factors include wide spread HIV; sex industry has established itself on a firm ground. Muslim militants in the south, keep on triggering problems to the government. Sometimes, occasional skirmishes take place along the borders of Cambodia on sovereignty of temples.

The most important issue that the country is facing is the quality of the political leadership. Does the country possess the fired up

and determined quality leadership? Are the government institutions geared up to high demands of efficiency and productivity? Is the government taking into stock the necessities of meeting the unexpected military situations? Is there a focused foreign policy? These are some of the most pertinent questions that are to be probed in depth. In the twenty first century, no country could ignore the importance of interconnected alignments with other nations as well as defining very sharply its own national interests. The economic progress is fundamental from every point of view; corrupt leadership, lack of bold visions and inexperience in governing practices become the major causes for the downfall of a nation. We project that Thailand in the next five years, will make steady progress but spectacular growth will be hard to achieve.
Note: Military has staged a coup (2014) and is in charge.

Philippines

Philippines: It is a country of seven thousand islands but only eleven are habitable; the rests of them are just mountainous and volcanic. It has a very large reserve of Gold and Copper. Ruled by the Spanish for almost three hundred years; it got its independence in 1946 from the United States after fifty years of occupation. It is a Catholic country with a population around one hundred million. The Gross National Income is below $3k per capita. In the early sixty and seventies, it made good economic progress. Electronic goods, electrical machinery, petroleum products, timber and textile were the main exports. Philippines is a popular tourist destination and is a strong ally of the United States.

The recent history of the country is not very encouraging from the point of view of economic progress and government transparency. Starting from 1965, when President Marcos became the president-he ruled the country for twenty years-followed by Estrada and President Ms Gloria Arroyo, Philippines was plagued by endemic corruption and incompetent governance. All the three ex presidents were charged for fraud and embezzlement of government money. Billions of dollars were pocketed by Marcos and his family when the country was facing dire poverty and high unemployment. It is irony that the general public could not change the situation quickly and the country has to suffer, subsequently.

It is very essential for any country to have stable and efficient governing institutions, supported by modern day business community to create jobs and business expansion; unfortunately this important aspect of growth and future prosperity is missing in Philippines at this junction. The present President Benigo Noynoy Aquino, son of popular President Ms Cory Aquino has said: Where there is no corruption, there is no poverty. It is true that corruption snatches away the growth but competency in governing is also very vital for economic progress. Energized leadership to lead the country is so important; continuous efforts are needed.

Millions of Philippines citizens have left because there are very few jobs available in the country. Statistics show that remittances from these migrants exceed the foreign direct investment. The population is exploding and if the government does not take very drastic measures, it could result in severe social unrest.

Philippines is facing two internal threats; Muslim militants linked with Al Qaeda in the southern region notably Mindanao, have staged frequent demonstrations demanding independence from the country. With the help of the United States military personnel, the uprising against the government has been put down but Mindanao is almost an autonomous state. In the north, Mao's organization is giving problem to the government. With the rise in poverty, sex trade is establishing its roots and it might be difficult to dislodge it from the community.

The present President, Benigno Noynoy Aquino has the advantage of iconic family reputation and he himself is known for his anti-corruption stand. He can transform the present dismal plight of the country's economic stagnation and move in the right direction. Philippines is a member of ASEAN and APEC and has signed an agreement of Free Trade with China. It does have the protection of the United States and therefore should not spend money on military build up. Setting up good high caliber educational institutions, creating an environment of business growth and bringing in large foreign investments with quick government decisions, will surely change the direction of the sleeping country. South Korea is a shining example in this respect.

Analyzing from different aspects- socio-economic and political- it is apparent that the country is facing huge dimensional challenges and unless the course is not changed now, it will become more difficult to do so later on. The poverty is on the rise, the population is exploding, jobs are disappearing, crime rate is going up, militants are getting stronger and corruption is spreading all over the society. Under this frightening scenario, where does the country stand? Strong leadership and dedicated army of efficient government officials can change this situation but it will not be an easy task. It will demand sacrifices from all.

The coming five years will show explicitly where the country is heading to? Progression or Recession! Once again, it could be said very truly that it is the youth of the country that assesses and changes the destiny of a country no matter what the circumstances might be. Philippines has all the potentials to be a prosperous country if the conditions are addressed in the right directions.

Conclusion
Five year Projections

We shall conclude our study by providing five year projections related to economic growth and political environment for each country. These projections have been made through available historical data and analysis of prevailing conditions. The task of interpretation of existing information does involve many sided variables which could change, depending upon future events; in other words some variance is inevitable. We have categorized these selected twenty countries into three distinct classes; the Top, the Medium and the Bottom.

A special section entitled Outlook for Scandinavian countries which include Norway, Sweden, Finland and Denmark is included which provides some insight into Utopian society; an in depth analysis of economic, social and political conditions of these countries are explored to compare with other existing systems.

Top Countries
U.S.A; China; Japan; Germany; France; United Kingdom

The greatest economy of the world brings forth the name of the United States of America; the Gross Domestic Product is hitting sixteen trillions. At this point the country is facing lot of financial problems; recession of 2008, the crisis of sub prime mortgage, failure of well established financial institutions, big budget deficits, high unemployment rates and other economic woes have brought about a negative growth of 3.5 % in GDP in 2009. A massive Stimulus package of 787 Billions from the President Obama restored some stability in the market. The economy has started moving up erratically; in 2013 the growth rate in GDP hit almost 3.4%. The inflation remained lower at 3.2 % but the unemployment figures are still high at 6.5%. The year 2014 is looking better from economic point of view; more jobs are being created and the world economy is improving. We are expecting a growth rate around 3 % this year; for the next five years, it seems that the U.S economy will grow at the average of 2.5% or even more. China is still going strong which is good for U.S.A.

There is no doubt about the political stability of the country; however, there are doubts whether the Republicans would come out winners in the coming elections of 2016. The remaining last two years of President Obama might give some hints. The Democrats are up in popularity regarding Mexican Immigration Laws, Fair Pay of minimum ten dollars an hour, Equal wages for women and controversial Health Insurance Program. Eight million Americans have signed up for Obama health care; it is a significant step in the right direction. It seems like that the Republican Party has become a party of exclusive wealthy people; has shown empathy towards poor and middle class families and as such could be considered as retrograde and anti-progress. However, after eight years of Democratic stronghold, the general public might like to see new faces of the Republicans in 2016.

.CHINA

The impressive progress made by Communist China is unparallel in world history; 300 million people have been pulled out from dire poverty, just in three decades-it is some achievement that any country could be proud of. It is also true that the negative background of this phenomenon is that the Chinese government owns everything and nobody can say any thing against the government; there is no freedom of speech or action. Judging by Chinese example, Communist Russia could not transform itself as the Communist China did. The growth rate of Chinese economy has been phenomenal; hitting 10%. Due to downturn in the global economy, the projected growth in 2014 is around 7.5%.

How China would look like in the near future, say five years from now? It is not difficult to perceive. With the spread of wealth among the masses and stability in the country, the chances are that there would be more freedom for the common man in the Chinese political structure. The rigidity may loosen up a little bit but do not expect any major changes. The Chinese democratic dictatorship is not going away, for a long time to come. Gradually, the leaders of China will start appreciating the values of personal freedom and human nature. China has a flourishing history going back to five thousand years and at present it is making tremendous efforts to change a poor and agricultural country to become a giant industrial empire. The society is changing fast but it will take some time before we could expect some drastic changes. It will have very rich people along with a sizeable chunk of poor and unemployed section of the population. China and India have huge population; in both countries, poverty, malnourishment and illiteracy will continue to prevail for a long time to come.

JAPAN

The third largest global economy is currently undergoing some tough time. Japan's public debt, proportion to its GDP is one of the highest among world's economies. The other important factor that is besetting the Japanese economy is a lingering stagflation for many years. The GDP is moving erratically from positive territory to the negative. During 2002 to 2007, it grew by 1.8%; in 2008, it was negative 1.2% and in 2009 it went down drastically to negative 6.3%. It rose sharply to positive 4.1% in 2010 but went down to negative .9 % in 2011. This trend of ups and down is moving along 2012 to 2014. It gives an indication that the economy is fluctuating based upon exports and internal consumption. The present Prime Minister of Japan Shinzo Abe is trying to prop up the economy by providing incentives to the consumers to spend as to stop stagflation and at the same time has raised the sales tax to reduce the public debt. His program has so far produced positive results but will it be the ultimate solution? Time will show. The next five years do not point out spectacular gains in GDP; if the global economy moves forward, Japanese share of exports will rise too and that would be a positive factor.

The next five years in the Japanese political arena, would be different from the past; it would usher in some dynamic changes. Prime Minister Abe wants to see Japan play a more active role in the global political settings. He does want to make changes in the Constitution which could allow the Japanese government to increase the military build up. The Chinese threat on South China Sea islands has provoked not only the Japanese but other South Asian countries like Philippines, Malaysia and Viet Nam have opposed the Chinese assertion. The United States has shown its solidarity by sending additional ships to Japan. Very recently, Japan has signed a comprehensive agreement with Australia and in 2014, the King and the Queen of Japan paid a visit to India. It gives some indication that Japan wants to strengthen the relations with these two South East Asian countries. It must be taken for granted that neither Japan nor China will engage in any kind of active war for exercising sovereignty on these islands. The stakes are much bigger than oil and gas that may or may not be there. China knows very well the consequences if it antagonizes the U.S.

GERMANY

The largest economy of Europe and the fourth largest of the world, Germany with 3.5 trillion Gross Domestic Product, is the best hope for staggering economies of Greece, Spain, Portugal and other similar countries where high unemployment rate and negative growth are creating lot of problems. When the global recession of 2008 was hitting almost all the countries, Germany had to rescue its faltering banks and pump in billions in Stimulus Program to survive the crash. In 2009, it had a negative GDP of 5.1% but it recovered in 2010 when it rose to positive 3.6%. Germany has a low inflation and the lowest unemployment rate in Europe. It seems like that 2014 will be a good year for economic growth world wide; in that scenario Germany may very well hit a growth rate of 3% or more.

In the next coming elections, Chancellor Angela Merkel may not be holding this position; in the past, she had been a pillar of strong support to the European solidarity-European Union and Eurozone. The next Chancellor might not follow her policies and endorsements. That might be a shift in the next five years. Some kind of resentment exists among German people for providing financial bail out to distressed economies of Europe. At this point it seems that it is in the interest of Germany to provide support to other European nations because a financial stable Europe stimulates the German economy. The political picture regarding bilateral and multilateral relations with France, England, U.S.A, China and other countries would remain more or less the same with no drastic changes in the next five years.

FRANCE

: It is the second biggest economy of Europe with $2.6 trillion Gross Domestic Product. In 2007, GDP rose by 2.2% but ended in negative territory in 2008 and in 2009 it stood at negative 2.6%. With the help of Stimulus program, the GDP went up by 1.4% in 2010; however, the budget deficit was 7% up, in sharp contrast to 3% GDP, as mandated by the European Union. The public debt in 2010 was up to 84% from 64% of Gross Domestic Product. The country is facing high unemployment rate ranging from ten to twelve percent; the younger generation is finding it more difficult to find jobs when the unemployment rates are hovering over twenty two percent. It is a serious problem.

President Hollande's policies for creating thousand of new jobs, increasing taxes on the wealthy, decreasing the budget deficits and growing economy have failed to materialize so far; consequently, he had to replace his Prime Minister and is trying to change the situation. If he does not take some drastic steps, French economy might go down and it may be replaced by the British. The next five years are crucial for the French economy. The public does not want any austerity program but at the same time if there is no sizeable growth in the economy, it does not spell good times. How the global economy takes shape, will be a decisive factor for France.

We see some slight political changes coming to French Republic in the direction of European Union. Like Germany, France will continue to support the solidarity of European nations but there would be change in the degrees of support; German economy is still going strong while the French economy is growing slowly and chances of its hitting more than 2.2% are not in the corner. A bright spot is that China had a 7.5% upward GDP in 2014 first quarter; that may help the French exports to China. The Russian economy will be in doldrums because of the recent crisis in Ukraine and the whole of the Middle East is drowned in its own local troubles and has no surplus money to import goods from outside. The recent elections of 2014 in India may bring a new government headed by Mr. Narendra Modi who might help raise the growth to 7% or more and that would also help the French economy to move up because France and India have established good trade relations that include military supplies, nuclear reactors and Air bus aircrafts. President Hollande may not be able to increase the taxes or cut the social programs but he has to pump in more stimulus money in the economy to move the French economy going forward. More jobs have to be created for the young.

The cordial relations that exist between France, Germany and the United States will continue to be strengthened. President Putins actions regarding Ukraine have jeopardized the channels of close relations between Russia and the West. The world does not want a repeat scenario of the Cold War that prevailed after World War II. A peaceful world, only, can bring in prosperity and happiness to all of us. Leaders of all the nations should work towards that goal.

GREAT BRITAIN

The sixth largest economy of the world with $2.4 trillions GDP ran into similar situation financially, as did the United States in 2008. The GDP dipped to negative 4.4% in 2009 but recovered to positive 1.8% in 2010. The British government had to pump in some $200 billions into Bank of England account to stabilize banking system in the country. The inflation rate is low around 2% and interest rates are as low as .5%. In 2014, the economy might grow at 2.5%. A bullish outlook is forecast for the economy and it is projected that it might take over the French bench number. It is expected that the global economy is going to grow in 2014 which would have a positive affect, worldwide.

According to the existing conditions, we see some changes coming along in two distinct areas, in the coming five years. The most pressing problem that England has to resolve is its relationship with the European Union. David Cameron, the Present Tory Prime Minister has announced that a referendum would be held which might help in deciding where England wants to go-leading to closer relations or somewhat loose connections. The chances are that British people would like to maintain their independent status rather than become a binding member of the European Union. It will be Germany and France which would be in the forefront of establishing more solid interconnecting policies rules and regulations and not England.

After more than sixty years of World War II, allies and Axis powers have established cordial and friendly relations among themselves. However, certain factors remain lingering on. The recent history shows amply that the United States and England are very well connected with each other and the future relations point out the same direction. In order of some precedence France and Germany come in second place and Italy and Russia could be grouped in the next circle. It must be remembered that blood relations are very important; in that context, England, Australia, New Zeeland and Canada holds very special relationship amongst them. The next five years would also see closer relations with India. British and Indians go along quite smoothly. Almost two million people of Indian origin have a big impact on the British way of life. Spicy dishes are number one choice, now.

ITALY

The land of the Roman civilization has seen many ups and downs in its history; at this juncture, it seems it will be moving in the right direction in terms of growth and prosperity. The new Prime Minister of Italy, the former mayor of Florence, Mr.Rizvi is the youngest political figure to hold this position. Many hopes have been built around him; that he is going to clean up the existing mess of mismanagement and corruption in the government structure. The country and the business community have been suffering from the amnesia of negative growth and self interest. With a S2 trillion Gross Domestic Product, it has been lagging behind other European countries in terms of growth. The unemployment rate is hitting more than ten percent and the budget deficit is hovering around 4.5%. The public debt is 120% GDP; inflation however, is low at 1.5%. With these figures, the new Prime Minister has to put an aggressive plan to reverse the existing conditions. If the new administration cut out the corruption and set up an efficient governing system, there is no reason that Italy could not achieve higher growth and excellent financial foundation. The next five years would be crucial for the Italian economy; it will be a question of do or die. If the right steps are being taken, the economy might go up by 1% in 2014 and may go up further down the road if the progress is maintained on a continuous basis. The government has to cut down the budget deficits as well as the public debt by implementing the appropriate plans. At the same time, it is also important to understand that the economy has to grow, so that the unemployment figures should go down which will bring a plateau of economic stability. In terms of building political relations with other countries, Italy will be a strong part of the European community. Business with China and India will grow as well with the Middle Eastern countries.

Italy is endowed with such a glorious history that tourist industry would have no problem in thriving and achieving higher degree of customer appreciation. Venice, Rome and Vatican have become a must for a tourist. Italian auto industry and fashion design groups would continue to bring in more business and no doubt, affordable wines and varieties of cheese would always keep the tourists happy. We see a bright future for Italy
.

CANADA

Canada is a member of North America Free Trade Association (NAFTA); United States is its biggest trading partner. The Gross Domestic Product is $1.8 trillion; the public debt ratio to GDP is the lowest. Inflation is 1.8% and it had a positive budget surplus till 2008. The GDP stood at positive 1.8% in 2001; went up to 3% in 2005. As the global recession hit in 2009, the GDP figures were negative 2.8% but it rose to positive 3.2% in 2010. It is expected that the economy will grow in 2014 and GDP may go up to 3%. The interest rates will not rise and the inflation would continue to be low. The next five years, in economic terms look fine; an average growth of 2.5 % is expected for Canada.

Canada has become a favorite country to immigrate for Asians especially Indians because almost two million people of Indian origin already live there and they have established themselves very well in the Canadian society. The present Prime Minister Steve Harper is very much enthusiastic in promoting good relations with India. When we look at Canada in terms of economic and political point of view, it is not difficult to project a prosperous and influential country emerging in the next five years. The next door neighbor, the United States would continue to be a solid partner in most of the economic and political relationship. The local Canadians would be more receptive to other cultures and point of views of other countries; in other words the society would be more liberal, flexible and forward looking.

.INDIA

The largest democracy of the world with a Gross Domestic Product of $1.8 trillion was moving fast till 2010. In 2005, the GDP rose to 9%; it went to 10% in 2007 and again in 2010, the growth rate registered 10%. For the last couple of years, the growth rate has fallen down to 5%. With a population of 1.2 billion people, India needs at least 7% rate of growth to generate ten million jobs which are needed to keep it moving in the right direction. Whosoever wins the 2014 election, this requirement has to be fulfilled otherwise there would be trouble for the country. The country has gone through high inflation rate of 12% in 2010; however, it has gone down to seven percent in 2013.

A country which is facing lot of problems on many fronts like poor infrastructure, acute shortage of power supply, lack of first class health system, illiteracy and rampant corruption at every stage of public administration, needs a strong and efficient leadership in all walks of life. The future looks not so bright under these conditions unless the right policies and systems are put in place. The younger generation is looking for these changes.

If we were to paint the present scenario of India on a cultural note, we can say without hesitation that the country is getting more westernized; however, the old traditions and values are still holding good. It seems like an amalgam of both is churning, in the present day Indian society. Trends are moving in the right direction and changes could be seen all over the country. It means progress; it is not going backward which is a good sign.

When we analyze the political picture of India in the coming five years, we see a definite indication that the country will be moving closer to the United States, Canada and England. Relations with Australia and Japan will be enhanced. China and Pakistan will continue to be considered hostile and unfriendly. Russia has lost its original place and would be considered as an ally but not very close. The Middle Eastern countries would remain on the side lines. Stronger friendly ties with Burma, Thailand, Bangladesh and Sri Lanka are good possibilities.

BRAZIL

One of the largest democracies of the world and the biggest economy of South America, Brazil has great potential to become a Super Power. The present population is just over two hundred million and the Gross Domestic Product is around $2.4 trillion. The unemployment rate is low at 6.4%; the inflation has really been tamed down to 5%. The public debt is projected at 48% GDP and the Gross National Income is $11k per capita. The country is rich in iron ore, newly discovered off shore oil reserves, plenty of Coffee beans and the largest producer of Ethanol. After facing financial debacles of the past-it paid off 15 billions to I.M.F two years ahead of time in 2005-and burying the 1000% inflation rates and getting rid of the military junta rule which lasted from 1964-

1985, Brazil is on its way to greater prosperity and economical stability. A member of BRICS group that include Brazil, Russia, India, China and South Africa, it is voicing for its right place in the global politics that includes becoming a permanent member of the Security Council. Brazil is going to stage the Olympic Games in 2016 and International Football Games will be taking place in 2014. Great cities of Rio de Janerio and Sao Paulo are brimming with construction activities of sporting stadiums. With all these positive activities taking place in the country, the government has to solve the pressing problem to provide housing facilities to thousands of slum dwellers who live in Favellas in the heart of major cities. The infrastructure needs immediate improvements to facilitate business growth and export business as well as increased tourists industry. It is going to make the difference.

Brazil is a country of big divide between the super rich and the real poor who have no place to live and no job to support the family. A powerful movement from Landless Rural Workers Party called MST had been going on for decades; it wants the government to intervene and legislate the re distribution of the land to the needy and the poor. The most popular President of Brazil, Lula de Silva, has done a great job in lifting millions of poor people from poverty by implementing his social programs. The present President, Ms Dilma Rousseff who was the chief Assistant to President Lula, is trying her best to remove corruption which is rampant in the country as well as provide an efficient governing system. The country is carrying a heavy baggage of poor health system and lack of excellent education institutions.

In spite of some major short comings in the government set up, the country is moving along well. A growth rate 0f 7.5 % in 2010 gives a good indication where the country is heading to. As long as the top brass in the government could curtail down the prevailing environment of corruption and implement strong social reforms to pull out a large section of the society from the existing unacceptable conditions of poverty and unemployment, Brazil will move in the right direction and one day will take its deserve place in the community of world nations. Brazil must equip itself with a strong group of professional business managers who could take the country forward. Along with that it is essential that the political leadership has to have some high levels of Goals and Objectives.

MEXICO

The second largest economy of Latin America is facing the major problem of drug trafficking. It is a very thriving business, running into billions of dollars. Mexico has become the major supplier source of all the drugs that are being sold in the United States and Canada. The drug cartels have become the greatest threat to peace and orderliness in the country similar to countries like Afghanistan and Pakistan where murders and bomb blasts are the routines of the normal day life. The difference is that in place of drug kings, it is the Islamic militants who have created fear and insecurity in the society. The government of the United States is providing monetary as well as military help to the Mexican government to eradicate the problem of drug trade but it is not an easy task. Unless the existing poverty situation is changed, this problem will not go away. That means heavy investment from the Unites States and other countries is very desirable. The country is beset with other problems too; there is high corruption in all areas of governing system and then there is shortage of experienced professional executives and business managers.

Mexico has large resources of oil and gas and now it has established a fairly good manufacturing base. If the top leadership utilizes its resources efficiently, the country could achieve high productive rates. The growth rate of GDP in 2010 was hefty 5.4%; the inflation rate was low at 4.1%. It is no denying the fact that a country moves forward when there is dedication and determination to make things happen, from the top leadership as well as general community as such. Considering all factors, the next five years for Mexican economy are not very rosy; however, it is expected that the economy will grow by 2.5% or so.

AUSTRALIA

It has earned the reputation as one of the most desirable countries of the world to live in-plenty of space, as big as the United States, clean, safe, very low unemployment with all the modern day amenities, available to the common man and woman of the country. With only twenty million people, the economy has reached $1.5 trillion. It is endowed with huge mineral wealth; iron ore, coal, oil and gas, copper, aluminum, Nickel, gold, diamonds and Uranium along with other products like wheat, wool, wines and meat have made the country a very resourceful place. The Gross National Income is $59K per capita. The average person has a pretty good living. The country has been running with a surplus budget till very recently and even in 2008 when the whole world was facing recession and financial crisis, the Australian economy grew by 2.4%.; in 2009, it went down to 1.5% and in 2011, it went up to 2.1%. Inflation in 2009 was 1.8% and in 2011, it went up to 2.8% .In 2014 the economy may go up by 2.2% or more depending upon how China and India move along. The next five years for Australian economy is looking good; its mineral wealth is the driving force. The dream idea of Prime Minister Kevin Rudd of making a bigger Australia is achievable; the Vision is right. All the desirable resources are available in the country but it would need grit and determination to make it happen.

Australia is surrounded by emerging and comparatively poor countries; no wonder citizens of other countries want to seek asylum or use illegal methods to come to Australian shore. The present Prime Minister Mr.Abbot is very much against the policy of allowing the citizens of other countries to move in. Looking from the example set up by the United States, it is clear that the foreign immigrants have created more jobs and improved over all growth and productivity. If the immigration policy is laid out properly and fairly, it is bound to go in favor of Australia, no doubts about it. Leadership has to have bigger Vision.

SOUTH KOREA

One of the poorest countries of the world in 1950 was South Korea. Now, see the transformation, South Korea is listed among the 15th richest countries in the world, in 2014. It has come a long way. Companies like Samsung, Hyundai, Kia, and L.G have established themselves very well in the global business world. These family owned business groups called Chaebol should be given due credit for it. It is also true that these interconnected business families have created an environment of corruption and bribery in the government circle. However, the overall direction leans towards more prosperity and growth for the Korean economy. It is interesting to note that with all this progress the country has made, 3% of population migrate to the United States, every year. Obviously, there are more opportunities in the United States than any other country for people who want to work hard and smart. South Korea is a shining example of shag to gold.

The economy of South Korea is very much linked with the United States, Japan, China and Australia. It has signed an agreement of Free Trade with the United States in 2012. Along with close business dealings, South Korea is relying heavily on United States to continue protecting the country from unpredictable dictatorial regime of North Korea. The present President of South Korea, Ms Park Chung hee, has taken a hard line approach towards North Korea's nuclear program. But

Sunshine policy is still being followed whereby families of North and South Korea are allowed to meet with each other.

The downturn that overshadowed the whole world economy in 2008, affected the South Korean growth to some extent. The Gross Domestic Product in 2008 grew by 2.3% but it went down to .3% in 2009 but recovered handsomely to 6% in 2010. It is estimated that South Korean economy will grow in the range of 4.5% in 2014. The next five years point out future growth and expansion unless the global geo economic conditions take a drastic reverse course of action. China is still in expansion mode and hopefully Indian economy will also start the growth engine after the new government in New Delhi takes control. Korea is a success story

.

TURKEY

With the exception of Lebanon, the most westernized Muslim country in the world is Turkey. The constitution does not tell that it is an Islamic country; the secular state is guaranteed and upheld by the law and in the past the military has taken its responsibility to see that religion and the government institutions are not mixed up in any way. Turkey came into existence in 1920 when the Ottomans Empire was disintegrated; Kamal Ataturk was the person who made this happened. With a population of 75 million people consisting of Sunnis and Shiite Muslims along with a small minority of Christians, the Gross National Income is around 11K per capita. The literacy rate is high at more than 90% -male and female. It is a member of NATO but not a member of the European Union which it has been trying for more than a decade. Luckily, Muslim militants group like Al Qaeda and Taliban have not established their stronghold in the country. The present Prime Minister Mr.Erdogan and the President Mr.Gul belongs to Justice and Development party which has its Islamic roots.

Turkey is not endowed with Oil and Gas reservoirs and it is not highly industrialized. One fifth of its GDP comes through the agricultural sector; textile, clothing, carpets, auto and electronic parts are sizeable export items. Tourist industry is also thriving well. Istanbul and Ankara are two popular tourist attractions. The GDP in 2007 grew by 4.7%, it went down to .7% in 2008 and in 2009 it dropped down to -4.8% but it recovered in 2010 and registered growth of 9.0%. It is expected that the economy will grow by 3-4% in 2014. The next five years will follow the same trend. The inflation rates were hovering around 8.6% in 2010 and in 2014 it is projected that it will be below 10%. The country has a minority of Kurdish people who want a separate state; at present they have agreed to a political truce with the government. We are projecting Turkey as a stable, increasingly prosperous and perhaps more influential country in the Muslim world. It will not be able to join the European Union as a regular member. However, it is in the interest of the western countries to keep Turkey on its side.

MALAYSIA

The country could boast of a healthy growth on a continual basis. In 1970, fifty percent of the population was below poverty line but in 2014, it is only six percent or even less. Like many emerging countries, it started as an agricultural economy but during the time when Dr. Mahathir was the Prime Minister (1981-2003), it was transformed into a giant manufacturing base. Electronics, telecommunication and auto parts are major items of exports now. Malaysia is also a rich resource for oil and gas. Palm oil, rubber and tin are sizeable foreign exchange earners. Along with plenty of agricultural and mineral resources, the country has 25% population which is Chinese Malaysians. The Chinese community has established successful businesses and has become the richest section of the Malaysian society. That has become a sore debating point in Malaysian politics though it is true that the local Muslim Malaysians literally run the government. Lately, the present Prime-Minister Mr.Razak has been telling the Malaysian people that these discriminatory laws have to change. The chances are that the local Muslim Community called Bhumiputra will not easily give up their assigned role of privilege, in the near future. The Malaysian economy is looking bright and more prosperous

The Gross Domestic Product grew by 6.5% in 2007; it declined to 4.8% in 2008 and took a nose dive to -1.6% in 2009. But it recovered in 2010 and registered a growth of 7.2%. Agriculture accounts for 8% of GDP. It is projected that for the next five years the average growth in GDP will be in the range of 5-6 %. Export for Oil and gas, palm oil and electronic parts will keep the economy humming. Malaysia has shortage of workers, so foreign workers from Indonesia and India are in demand. Malaysia is not a conservative Muslim country like Saudi Arabia but it must be noted that any comment against Koran or Prophet Mohammad is not tolerated and is punishable by law. The Western culture is not embraced by the general public; strict Muslim traditions are the norms. However, things are changing gradually. In 2014, President Obama made a short visit to Malaysia and signed some agreements related to trade and military co operation. This is a turning point in Malaysian politics. Dr.Mahathir was a strong opponent of American policies; the Present Prime Minister Mr.Razak is changing the course. It will be interesting to watch how he does it.

INDONESIA

Indonesia is a member of 20G, group of twenty industrialized countries of the world. Though countries like Afghanistan and Pakistan are riddled with Taliban and Al Qaeda, Indonesia, the largest Muslim country is not a stronghold of Islamic militants. It is a moderate Muslim country where the Constitution gives full freedom to every one to follow his/ her own religious beliefs and traditions. Bali, a beautiful Indonesian Island is a Hindu state, even today. The country is rich in Gas and Oil, Palm oil, rubber and tin; textiles, timber, auto parts and electrical appliances are big export items. Under President Suharto, Indonesia made impressive economic gains; an agricultural economy was transformed into a roaring industrialized society. The country is facing many challenges which include corruption, poverty and old infrastructure. The plus point is that the literacy rates are high at 92%. Agriculture contributes 12% to GDP and about 40% people are employed in this sector. Japan is one of the major investors in Indonesian economy. Relations with China, India, Malaysia and Thailand are close and as a member of Non Aligned Nations and ASEAN, Indonesia is playing an important role in world politics.

The Gross Domestic Product during the period of 1992-96 grew by 7.6% and in 2007 and 2008 it was up by 6%. Even at the time of global recession in 2009, the GDP rose by 4.6% and in 2010, it went up to 6.1%. It is a remarkable achievement. The inflation rate in 2009 was 4.8% and it rose to 5.1% in 2010; once again it showed the strength of the economy; the unemployment was low at 8.4% in 2008 but it went up in 2014. These figures of GDP show that the Indonesian economy is heading in the right direction. We can project that in 2014, when economies in China and India are taking a hit, Indonesia might pull ahead with a growth rate of 5%. The next five years for Indonesia are looking good in terms of growth and future prosperity. In this context, it must be noted that corruption has to be curtailed in order to reach this status. The next President has to be a strong leader to root out the prevailing environment of bribery and palm greasing; it will not be an easy task to carry out but it has serious implications, if not done.

THAILAND

A country of seventy million people, Thailand has made steady progress economically since 1980; the Gross National Income is $5K. The people below poverty level in 1990 were 18 millions; now in 2014, they are less than five millions. The adult literacy rate is 95%. It is an export oriented economy; eighty percent of GDP comes through exports. Rice, timber, auto parts, electronic goods, textiles, oil and gas are the major export items. Japan is the leading investor in Thailand's economy. The country is still an agricultural society; 70% people lives in rural areas.

Thailand is undergoing a political crisis right now. For couple of years a political battle is going on between Ms Shinawatra supporters (PTP) and the opposition leader Vijjajiva who has the backing from the rich elite group as well as from the military establishment. In 2014, Prime Minister Shinawatra was forced by a Corruption court to resign and face many other charges. New elections are going to take place in the near future; the country is heading towards unstable conditions. It is bound to affect the economy in someway or the other. Intervention from the military has already taken place in 2014. Martial Law has been imposed and the Military Junta is running the country. It is also unfortunate that the political parties look towards their own personal agenda and ignore the needs of the country and its citizens. Under these prevailing conditions, Black market economy gathers momentum and the government loses its strength. It is estimated that 48% of GDP is hidden, in Thailand black market.

Looking from the GDP standpoint, it grew by 4% during 1999-2007; went down in 2008 to 2.6% and nose dived to -2.4% in 2009. It recovered in 2010 and went up by 7.8%. However, the recovery was not sustained in 2014. Considering political instability in the country and global economic situation, the next five years for Thailand's economy are not looking very bright. The export market will be weaker and the government would not be taking any bold decisions. It is projected that it might move ahead by 3-4%. There are so many uncertainties; however, the tourist industry which provides 6% of GDP will not be affected in any big way provided the country does not become unsafe for tourists. The country has all the potentials to achieve higher growth rates but it will require some strong leadership and determination to make it happen. Corruption and black money market have to go otherwise it would not be possible.

PAKISTAN

In 1930 a famous Muslim poet Mohammed Iqbal proposed the idea that a separate state should be created for Muslims because they can not live with Hindus. The politician Mohammed Ali Jinnah took up this idea and convinced the British government to partition India into two states-India and Pakistan. So in 1947 Pakistan was created; that division of India took a death toll of one million people-Hindus and Muslims. The history of our world has seen such kind of calamities with pain and anguish but that is how the life goes on. After more than sixty years, Pakistan is still rolling in turmoil and distress and safety of a common man and woman is a far cry, in this Islamic country. The government is helpless and crazy militia men keep up their Jihad and keep up exploding their bombs on a regular basis. The present Prime-Minister of Pakistan Nawaz Sharif is trying to make a deal with Pakistani Taliban so that the safety of a common citizen is restored in the country. It is unfortunate that a minority of people who are mostly uneducated with no jobs and who are also fanatic about their Muslim faith are dictating their terms and conditions to the so called silent majority of Pakistan. It seems like a situation where keeping silence may be the best alternative. This scenario is very well alive and strong in the neighboring country of Afghanistan, too. It will take a long time before things would change for better.

Where the country is heading in the next five years? It is not very difficult to predict. Pakistan can not get rid of these religiously blind people and the only course of action for the government would be to let them live their own way of life and spare the rest of the population from their crazy ideology.

The population of the country is exploding; it is expected that it will reach 189 million people in 2015. The largest Muslim country, Indonesia has a population of 250 million; India is number third with a Muslim population of 150 million people. It has been noted that the Muslim community has a higher rate of birth as well as lower literacy numbers and is lagging behind other societies.

Pakistan is an agricultural country; 20% GDP comes through agriculture. The Gross National Income is $2.5 K per capita. The inflation rate was 20.8% in 2009; in 2010, it was down to 11.7%. GDP in 2008 grew by 3.7%; it dipped down to 1.7% in 2009 but in 2010 it went up to 3.8%. The latest figures for 2014 GDP are projected to go up by 5%. This is not bad considering all the difficulties that the government is facing. The loan from the I.M.F and the U.S aid package has made the difference. Political instability, corruption on a large scale in all government dealings and lack of competent work force are the major hurdles for the country to overcome in order to move towards growth and prosperity. Strong leadership and friendly relations with India and other neighborly countries will really be very helpful.

PHILIPPINES

The history of economic progress in any country is based upon certain prerequisites which have to be in place; when we look at Philippines, we notice that those very essential requirements are missing. Since 1965, when President Marcos became the president, the country has been tainted with corruption; President Corazon Aquino is the only exception who was not charged for bribery, embezzlement and personal gains. The present president, Benigno Aquino has said in his speeches that where there is no corruption, there is no poverty. However, poverty is still a big issue and unemployment is forcing the people to migrate to other countries; there are around six million Philippine citizens who have already left the country to have a better life. Governing a country is just like running a company; experience is a must.

The next five years for Philippine economic growth do not look bright. The government has to start an aggressive plan to set up manufacturing industry in the country; provide attractive tax breaks and other incentives to the local business community as well as to the foreign investors. Creating jobs should become number one priority for the leaders of the country. Borrowing money from international resources like IMF and World Bank should be considered to set up tax free economic zones; along with this it is necessary to establish business training institutions to provide qualified personnel to run the manufacturing and service industries. At the present time, top executives are just not available. The economic environment is not conducive; it has to be changed and that will come only when the top leadership would make it happen through their efforts and unfailing dedication. In 2014, President Obama made a short trip to Philippines and signed agreements to strengthen military cooperation and provide some financial aid in the areas of education, health and agriculture. It should be noted that Philippines is an agricultural economy; 15% GDP comes through agriculture and around 40% people are employed in agricultural sector. GDP growth was 1.1% in 2009; but amazingly the GDP rose sharply in 2010 by 7.6%. It is projected that in 2014, the economy will grow by 2-3%. Free trade agreement with China will be a big factor.

RUSSIA

The largest country of the world and a super power in terms of military strength, Russia is still far behind the Western countries as far as the economic power is concerned. The gross national income for an average Russian is $11k whereas it is $40K for an ordinary citizen of Western Europe. More than sixty years have elapsed since the World War II ended but unfortunately the standard of living in today's Russia has not changed very much. Compared to Russia, China has transformed itself in a marvelous way.

President Putin an ex KGB-Secret Police-Intelligence Agent, was very much upset when 1n 1991, the mighty United Soviet Socialist Republic was disintegrated and all the countries over which Russia had the controlling voice became independent. He has expressed many times that it was the darkest hour in the history of Russia when this happened. He carries a grudge against the western powers to make it happen. In 2014, when Ukraine was undergoing trouble in the province of Crimea, he immediately rushed to pro Russian elements and within a month, Crimea became a Russian territory. Putin does not want any part of the so called Russian area of influence to come under the West. The western countries have started putting sanctions against Russia but things are not moving in the right directions.

The countries of Europe are dependent upon the supplies of Oil and Gas from Russia and that is the trump card that Mr. Putin is holding in his hands. It is irony of facts that Europe as well as Russia would be hurt if something goes wrong in this situation. It will depend upon President Putin to back off from his firm stand or let the western countries put a squeeze on Russian economy. It seems like that some kind of common ground would be found by both sides and this issue would go away. The long term prospects for Russian economy are not bad; export of military hardware; nuclear reactors and Oil and Gas will give a big boost to GDP.

The chances are that the progression in the Russian economy will be slow. The Russian governing institutions are still struggling with the principles of democracy and capitalistic society. The general public is not fully exposed to the fine tuned democratic structure and dictatorial and authoritarian way of running the government is still very much persisting with the Russian people. To turn a well oiled machinery of a Communist country to an efficient Capitalist utopia, is not an easy task; it will take its time.

Since Russia is armed to its teeth and is flooded with nuclear technology, it will continue to dictate the direction of global policies. However, the common man and woman of Russia will not be enjoying all the bounties of the modern day society in the near future, which are available to the Western countries as of now, This difference will persists for some time till the Russian government and the governing machinery change its course of actions. Russia was a poor country of Europe to start with; Lenin wanted to change it and Stalin wanted to conquer the world. What do we expect to see in the next five years in Russia? It is not difficult to predict-the country will move along slowly; we should not expect spectacular results and glorious outcomes and that is the projection, at this time.

When Ukraine picked up the headlines of the world news in 2014, Crimea which was previously a part of it and later joined the Russian Empire, the so called Cold War resurfaced again. Russia stands to lose economically and morally if it moves against the Western Powers because it is still far behind the European nations and the United States in all aspects. It might not be a bad idea for Russian leadership to learn something from the Chinese model of Communist cum Capitalistic system of running the government.

Outlook: Scandinavian Countries
Utopian Society

When we take a cursory look at Scandinavian countries-Norway, Sweden, Finland and Denmark-we are immediately struck with certain exclusive factors like small population and a well qualified work force; we should inquire how these nations established some of the most admired utopian societies? They have to be given high score for their ingenuity and vision; they have shown how government and its people could really transform the whole picture of life to a graceful and vibrant living. These countries enjoy highest standard of living and a long life to cherish. What else would you ask for? Yes, there are not many billionaires in these countries but there are many smiling faces.

Let us examine the data sheets for these countries. Norway has a population of five million people; the Gross National Income per capita is $98K, one of the highest in the world. The export figures for Oil and Gas have reached $40 billions per year. The country has established a Sovereign Fund of $400 billions- an amazing financial strength. Sweden has a population of ten million people; the Gross National Income is $55K per capita. The life expectancy is 80 years for male and 84 years for female-one of the highest longevity record in our planet. We move to Finland, next. The population is five million and the Gross National Income per capita is $50K. It is the country of Smart phone Nokia. Down in the south is Denmark which has a population of five million people. The Gross National Income per capita is $60K. All the four countries have excellent education, health and work related training program for all citizens. The saying: from the cradle to the last breadth, is supported and sustained by heavy personal and business taxes. The people in these countries are enthusiastic to create such a society where every one has a good chance to lead a happy life. These are super rich countries but they do not have mighty military power to rule over other countries.

While reviewing data on economic prosperity and population statistics, it is noticeable that countries with small population, like these four Scandinavian countries as well some other European countries like Holland Belgium, Switzerland and Austria, where the population is less than ten million people, have established very good standard of living for its citizens. No doubt, the other factors for this prosperity are manufacturing expertise, technical competency, business intelligence and modern scientific knowledge like Information technology and telecommunication. In this highly competitive world, the work force has to be well equipped with the latest and the greatest new techniques and gadgets. On the other side of the horizon when we look at countries with large population and not having these other required elements in their societies, there are grim chances of seeing high unemployment, low wages and no growth in their economies. Greece, Portugal, Spain and Ireland fall under this category. They say it is the quality of its people and not the quantity which would decide how you would live your life in those countries. This scenario is true for emerging Asian and African countries, too. Education, qualified trained workforce and smart business practices can take any country to a higher plateau.

These Scandinavian countries will continue to move towards more prosperity and growth; with newly found, off shore oil and gas wells, Norway would lead the way for others to build higher degree of industrialization in their respective countries. Not only that, these countries are playing active role in establishing peace in different regions of our world. Resolving conflict between Israel and Palestine and participating in peace keeping mission in Afghanistan through United Nations channel, are notable examples of Scandinavian countries playing their active role in world politics. Sweden has adopted a positive immigration policy towards Asian and other countries; it is estimated that ten percent of the population consists of foreign nationals, not born in Sweden.

Broadly speaking, we can define Utopian society as the one where all the citizens of the country have been guaranteed all the amenities which are necessary to lead a comfortable life, by the government. Like any business entity, the government has to run its functions based upon the expenses, expenditures and revenues it gets from all the sources. Let us explore the revenue side, first. There are four means or outlets which are available to the government to fund its treasury. They are: Collection of all Taxes-personal and business. Number two: Raising the Taxes to get more funds. Number three: Borrowing from the public through bonds. Number four: Taking loan from International Banks. Next, we shall see the expenditure side. The government can spend money on any selected social program that benefits its citizens like providing free education, free health or free technical training. It can establish subsidized programs to purchase food and other commodities to the general public to offset their financial burden. In all these situations, the government has to assess and evaluate the total revenues, net expenditures, debt and deficits and then formulate its policies.

It is not uncommon to see more of deficits and debts rather than more revenues and surplus budgets. In such scenarios what should be the role of the government? Should it increase its debt limits, let the budget deficits not close down the social welfare programs? These are crucial questions to address. If the government is running on surplus budgets, then there is no problem at all. But when the deficits and debts are rising, all the sides of the balancing acts have to be thought and looked at when it is planning to introduce its social programs. We have to take some clues from China, France, Japan and Brazil where the government kept their welfare programs in spite of higher national debts and budget deficits. President Obama is facing same problem in the United States where the Republican Party does not want to raise borrowing ceiling and wants to curtail all social welfare programs.

What are the possibilities for countries like India with huge population to attain some structure of a Utopian society for their country? Is it just a dream to come true or could it be made viable? There is no doubt that having a large poverty stricken population, a country can not achieve that status. A large population which is not wealthy and is just struggling to stand on its own resources would not be able to create such a society; however, if aggressive steps are taken in the right direction, it might not be impossible to build a sustainable structure to build shining welfare societies

A country like United States which has a large population and which is very rich too can join the Scandinavian Group; but the powerful elite group of the society does not want to create such a structure in the country. This philosophy of Capitalism draws not only criticism but also apathy and resentment for a good and desirable cause. It does not make any sense to think that the government should not do any thing to change the status quo for the poor and disadvantaged section of the society.

In our fast moving world, bold plans with calculated risks and flexible planning have to be taken by the government to start putting in place, the Scandinavian model of universal welfare programs, in stages. It will be difficult, may be impossible task to roll in a massive social program all in one step; gradual deployment will bring in sure success, without running into different kind of hurdles and obstructions. The successful implementation of universal welfare program will be strongly linked to the caliber of highly dedicated leadership of the country.

Most of the people in our world want peace, prosperity and happiness for all the residents of this planet. Universal welfare program for all the citizens, similar to the Scandinavian System, is a reliable result oriented plan to achieve this objective. It could be made possible if the leadership of the country is in the hands of competent, dedicated and fired up individuals who are also visionaries and free from corruption. It is a great goal to achieve.

Most of the Western European countries have established social welfare system for its citizens; it may not be comparable to the Scandinavian System which covers almost every aspect of life. United States of America is far behind in this race. It is only recently that President Obama introduced free health plan for general public and ironically Republican Party opposed it vehemently. It seems that Republicans have become retrograde in all directions. It is a matter of shame that one of the richest countries of the world does not offer free health services for its citizens. The rich elite group should be blamed for this.

If we look inquisitively at the entire spectrum of global progression, there are clear indications that the rich countries of the world were not involved seriously in moving the emerging poor countries of Asia, Latin America and Africa towards growth and economic advancement; Foreign Direct Investment and other financial aid programs did not make any substantial inroads into their economies and consequently disparities between the rich and poor countries continue to thrive.

It must be noted down that any country where corruption, lack of governing competency, absence of aggressive economic plans and no incentives for business growth prevails, the possibilities of establishing social welfare programs are very dim. A good working relationship between the government, business community and the workforce is an essential prerequisite for rolling out programs that benefits the lower stratum of the society. It is important to create an environment of consensus in the society that every citizen has the right to live a dignified and comfortable life and every body has to pitch in to make it happen; however, it is the government that has to take the leadership role. Scandinavian countries have shown the path of an enlightened roadmap for the world to follow its example. Some deviations in the planning process are bound to be there but the fundamentals should be kept in tact. Question: If we see   something desirable, why should not we embrace it?

Utopian Society versus Capitalism: The most powerful Capitalist country in the world is the United States of America; however, millions of people are poor and do not have means to go up in life because the national government does not guarantee its citizens the minimum facilities to lead a carefree living. On the other side, the Scandinavian society provides everything which is essential for a dignified way of life. In between the two extreme situations, most of the western countries of Europe like France, England, Germany and others do provide good safeguards and channels to its citizens so that they do not have to worry on day to day basis how they are going to lead their life. We can say that Communism and Socialism could be considered as the starting concept for establishing a Utopian society in a country.

In our study of twenty countries which include nuclear as well as non nuclear powers-U.S.A, France, England, Russia, China, India, Pakistan, Turkey, Indonesia, Philippines and Thailand-none of these countries fall into the category of Utopian societies. There are good chances that Japan, Germany, France, Switzerland and Austria may adopt the Utopian Model in not too distant a future for their citizens. Countries like India, Indonesia, China, Pakistan, Philippines and Thailand are not in a position to afford this luxury; it makes it clear that it is only rich countries that can reach this destination. U.S.A, Canada, England and Australia have the resources to establish good social welfare program for its citizens but it will be the public opinion that would make it happen.

A well rounded social welfare program can be established in a country only if the political leadership is fired up and dedicated to launch it. Support from all sections of the society is needed otherwise, it will run into troubles. In twenty first century the Utopian model could be rolled out universally if there is a will and determination; there are many resources which could be utilized to fund it. However, it is true everyone in the society has to share the responsibility with a smile; it is true: reaching the stars is not easy.

Suggested Readings

Why we need smart government for a strong economy by Bill Clinton. Publisher: Alfred Knoff, New York. 2011

Rivals: Power struggle between China, India and Japan by Bill Emmott. Publisher: Harcourt, Inc, New York. 2008

The elephant and the dragon-India and China-by Robyn Meredith Publisher: W.W. Norton & Co; New York. 2007

A brief history of Mexico by Lynn Foster, Publisher: Info-base Publishing, New York 2010

History of Italy by Charles Killinger, Publisher: Greenwood Press, Connecticut. 2002

A modern history of Japan by James McClain, Publisher: W.W. Norton & Co. 2002

Understanding China by John Starr, Publisher: Farrar, Straus and Giroux, New York.2010

China's Rise: Challenges and Opportunities by Bergsten Fred and Charles Freeman, Publisher: Peterson Institute of International Economics, Washington D.C 2008

Capitalism with Chinese Characteristics by Huang Yasheng, Publisher, Cambridge University Press, New York 2008

Culture and Customs of India by Carol Henderson, Publisher, Greenwood Press, Connecticut, 2002

In the line of Fire by Pervez Musharraf, Publisher, Free Press, New York, 2006

Pakistan and the emergence of Islamic Militancy by Hussain Rizvi, Publisher, Aldershot, Hamshire, England, 2005

Political Handbook of the World 2012.Editor: Tom Lansford. Publisher, Sage Press, Washington D.C

Imagining India by Nandan Nilekani; Publisher: Penguin Press, New York. 2009

The Statesman Year Book 2014, Publisher: Palgrave Macmillan.

Index